In It Together

In It Together

How Student, Family, and Community
Partnerships Advance Engagement and
Achievement in Diverse Classrooms

Debbie Zacarian
Michael Silverstone

CORWIN
A SAGE Company

FOR INFORMATION:

Corwin
A SAGE Company
2455 Teller Road
Thousand Oaks, California 91320
(800) 233-9936
www.corwin.com

SAGE Publications Ltd.
1 Oliver's Yard
55 City Road
London EC1Y 1SP
United Kingdom

SAGE Publications India Pvt. Ltd.
B 1/I 1 Mohan Cooperative Industrial Area
Mathura Road, New Delhi 110 044
India

SAGE Publications Asia-Pacific Pte. Ltd.
3 Church Street
#10-04 Samsung Hub
Singapore 049483

Acquisitions Editor: Dan Alpert
Associate Editor: Kimberly Greenberg
Editorial Assistant: Cesar Reyes
Production Editor: Cassandra Margaret Seibel
Copy Editor: Sarah J. Duffy
Typesetter: C&M Digitals (P) Ltd.
Proofreader: Susan Schon
Indexer: Jean Casalegno
Cover Designer: Michael Dubowe
Marketing Manager: Stephanie Trkay

Printed in the United States of America.

A catalog record of this book is available from the Library of Congress.

ISBN 978-1-4833-1677-2

This book is printed on acid-free paper.

15 16 17 18 19 10 9 8 7 6 5 4 3 2 1

Contents

Dedication and Acknowledgments

We express our gratitude to several individuals who contributed to this project. Many educators took time away from their busy schedules to read early drafts, provide suggestions, and let us know that we were on the right path to what they believe is sorely needed. Lydia Breiseth, manager of Colorín Colorado, graciously put us in touch with the American Federation of Teachers, and we reached out to exemplary colleagues including outstanding members of the ASCD and TESOL communities in our effort to provide a broad range of examples-in-practice from across the United States in urban, suburban, and rural settings. Thank you to the following teachers and specialists for doing just that: Kelley Brown, Darryl Clark, Angela Ghent, Susan Goldstein, Kristina Labadie, Louise Levy, Alicia Lopez, Keith Maletta, Elise May, Alexandra McCourt, Jennifer Melton, Ntina Paleos, Maureen Penko, Lucy Gable, Barbara Rothenberg, Sylvia Schumann, and Pam Snow.

Throughout, our editor, Dan Alpert, provided steadfast support, encouragement, and suggestions, including an external review process, which further strengthened the book. Cassandra Seibel and Sarah Duffy, from Corwin, polished our writing and made it shine. We are grateful to Corwin for their exceptional commitment and valuable support throughout the process, and we are especially grateful to Cesar Reyes and Kimberly Greenberg for their care and attention to details large and small throughout this effort.

We spent many hours on this project. A very special and heartfelt thanks goes to our spouses, children, and friends for their support throughout and for flexibility when deadlines loomed.

Last, but by no means least, the ideas for this book would not be possible without the inspiring students and inspired teachers we have known. We dedicate this book to them and to the families and communities that stand together to bring the ideals of equity, access, and engagement ever closer to possibility day by day.

Publisher's Acknowledgments

Corwin gratefully acknowledges the contributions of the following reviewers:

Christel Broady
Associate Professor, Graduate Education
Georgetown College
Georgetown, KY

Ayanna Cooper
Educational Consultant
Circle Dallas, GA

Andrea Honigsfeld
Professor
Molloy College
Rockville Centre, NY

Dorothy Kelly
Student Teacher Supervisor
Fontbonne University
St. Louis, MO

Jane Kerschner
Educator and Leadership Coach
Kaleidoscope Coaching and Consulting
Chevy Chase, MD

Katherine Lobo
Teacher (K–12) and Adjunct Professor
(undergraduate and graduate level)

Dr. Liliana Minaya-Rowe
Professor Emerita
University of Connecticut

Melissa Nixon
Director of Title I
Guilford County Schools
Greensboro, NC

Tamara Jo Rhomberg
National Literacy Consultant
Zaner-Bloser Company
Fenton, MO

About the Authors

 **Debbie Zacarian**, EdD is the founder of Debbie Zacarian & Associates, a business dedicated to advancing equity, access, and engagement of diverse student populations. She provides consulting, policy analysis and writing, strategic planning, and professional development to strengthen instructional practices, leadership, coaching, and parent-school partnerships.

Dr. Zacarian was the founding director of the Center for English Language Education and Advancing Student Achievement at the Collaborative for Educational Services, Northampton, Massachusetts, where she led various professional development initiatives for thousands of educators, wrote policies for the Massachusetts Department of Early Education and Care and many urban, suburban, and rural districts, including Boston Public Schools' programming for English learners, and consulted with the Massachusetts' Federation for Children with Special Needs and Parent Information Resource Center. For more than a decade, she served as clinical faculty at the University of Massachusetts-Amherst. In addition to service work, she designed and taught courses including Managing Culturally Responsive Classrooms and Developing Curriculum for the Heterogeneous Class. Dr. Zacarian was also the founding director of the Amherst Public Schools' English Learner and bilingual programs where she and the district received several state and national awards.

She has authored numerous publications, including *Mastering Academic Language: A Framework for Supporting Student Achievement* (2013); *The Essential Guide for Educating Beginning English Learners* (2012) with Judie Haynes; *Transforming Schools for English Learners: A Comprehensive Framework for School Leaders* (2011); and *Teaching English Language Learners Across the Content Areas* (2010) with Judie Haynes.

Michael Silverstone has been a full-time elementary teacher in Massachusetts since 1998. With Debbie Zacarian, he co-authored the Grade 2 chapter in *Academic Language in Diverse Classrooms: Promoting Content and Language Learning, Mathematics, Grades K–2* (Corwin). His essay recounting his discovery of the vital importance of maintaining professional autonomy while fostering relationships with students, families, and colleagues—in spite of all the pressures to standardize classroom practice—is the closing teacher essay in the anthology *Why We Teach Now*, edited by Sonia Nieto (Teacher's College Press). Silverstone is also the author of a number of young adult nonfiction books including *Rigoberta Menchú: Defending Human Rights in Guatemala* and *Winona LaDuke: Restoring Land and Culture in Native America* (The Feminist Press at the City University of New York). He is a teacher consultant with the Western Massachusetts Writing Project of the National Writing Project. http://www.umass.edu/wmwp/

Introduction

How do two separate people from different places and with different roles actually go about writing one sentence, let alone a book? Our answer takes some explaining as it reflects what we believe is needed in education now. The process of co-writing this book began, as many collaborations do, from talking. We met at a local coffee shop—one where there's free Wi-Fi, customers can linger as long as they want, and the aroma of hand-roasted coffee makes it easy to relax, sit and talk, and generate ideas. This wasn't our first experience in writing collaboratively. We had co-written a chapter in an edited series about academic language and found the experience to be powerful in terms of melding our ideas into a collective piece. It wasn't that we didn't see things differently at times. We each had our own points of view, which probably accounts for our ability to advocate tenaciously—a quality that could have been disastrous to our writing partnership if it weren't also paired with our habits as educators to listen and seek solutions for the greater good. Co-writing a chapter, we found, was as stimulating and thought provoking as it was a complicated and circuitous process. Our willingness to listen to and value each other's divergent views helped to expand our individual and collective thinking and work. When we had different views (and we did often) or weren't sure how to proceed, we stopped the writing process and didn't start up again until we had a clear idea of how to truly factor these in to go forward. These stop, reflect on each other's ideas, agree/disagree, and come to agreement experiences are emblematic of what we believe is urgently needed in education.

We're in a time of dramatic changes in education, but when it comes to the struggles of Latinos, African Americans, Alaskan Natives and indigenous Americans, English learners, and students living in poverty, little has changed for decades regarding how badly school is going. While new accountability standards and teacher and administrator evaluation systems are challenging every educator in unprecedented ways, the sheer number of students from these under-represented populations (they are predicted to be the majority population by 2020) should instantly raise our level of alarm. However, we believe the amount of time that's being focused on understanding and making these regulations and initiatives work is sapping the energy to do what is really most needed: to make education truly work for the very groups that it is not currently working for. This is not a new battle cry.

In 1988, Lisa Delpit, renowned for her scholarly contributions in education, gave a speech titled "The Silenced Dialogue: Power Pedagogy in Educating Other People's Children" at the ninth annual Ethnography in Education Forum. In it, she called for us to listen, really listen, and value different perspectives. To do this, we have to be willing to learn with and from each other in this important work. In addition, Delpit called for educators to embrace the diversity that is occurring in our classrooms and simultaneously support students from these diverse cultural, racial, economic, and linguistic backgrounds to be successful in school. To do the latter, we believe, requires taking the time to really sort through what it means to be a successful learner. What do we mean by successful? Being a successful student in today's schools means having the skills, competencies, and confidence to be active in the knowledge acquisition process, being a full member of the learning community in which this is occurring, and having the capacity to express oneself successfully in school, on state tests, and beyond—all the while learning to be an independent and critical thinker. We believe that change is possible only when we (students, teachers, families, the school community, and the community at large) are all in it together, working collaboratively to ensure that education works for everyone. In other words, teaching does not rest with teachers alone; it is a collective responsibility that works when everyone is active and welcomed and where interactions, and lots of them, are constantly encouraged and promoted.

So how two authors come up with one text is akin to how educators, students, and families must come together. For this introduction, for example, Debbie would send Michael a draft of her thoughts. Michael would write back, "What if we said [this and that thing I'm burning to say]?" Debbie might then say, "Okay, when we do this, how will we be sure that we also include . . . ?" The roles were reversed numerous times during the project and are characteristic of our writing process—to this minute!

Many drafts were written, each making us work harder, more precisely, and ultimately more efficiently at what became this final product. In the process, we came to know and value as well as challenge each other while at the same time trusting that what we wrote would be based on mutual respect and collaboration. Our process for creating this book was not just a model of authors' collaboration but also a depiction of the type of collaborative dynamic that is sorely needed in contemporary education.

As educators, our individual perspective, despite our most sincere and idealistic drive to bring out the best in our students, is missing something. It is always a partial picture of any whole and requires the contributions of others to be more complete. However, we believe that teachers have the pivotal role in fostering an open and much needed dialogue with students, families, the school community, and the community at large to ensure that education works. No one person or authority has the answers. Rather, when we invite and are open to what others bring, when we allow ourselves to be changed by different perspectives, and when we see these as gifts rather than obstacles to what we can achieve, then we can truly be in it together.

In this spirit, we called on many teachers from across the United States to furnish us with much-needed examples in practice. To articulate specifics and provide a practical roadmap for this work, we also infused several research-based preparation and instructional strategies to show how we can support learners from many different cultural, racial, linguistic, and economic experiences to be successful in school. The result of our collaborative efforts is a book that is dedicated to teachers and teachers in training who, like all of us in public education work, are experiencing the productive tensions of working with an increasingly diverse student population against a backdrop of regulatory initiatives. We believe strongly that we can make education work for all when we continually expand and develop our circles of collaboration to be truly in it together and that there is no better or more important time to do this than right now.

1

What It Means to Be "In It Together" in Education

No significant learning can occur without a significant relationship.

—James Comer

It's August and advertisements for school supplies and clothing begin as a trickle and eventually floods over the radio, television, Internet, and print media. For some 4 million U.S. educators, a once seemingly far-off day draws near. The new school year looms ahead like a mountain: in some ways inspiring and thrilling, in other ways supremely challenging, and even—dare we say—daunting. As teachers, teacher educators who prepare future teachers, or professional developers who support continuous learning to strengthen our practice, we hope that we know just what it means to try to foster our students becoming effective thinkers and caring members of our society, and to dedicate our care and determination to help to make their lives better and to be part of making our world better. It's what we do throughout the school year—continuously reevaluating and making adjustments about how to help all of our students to be successful.

Teaching has never been a simple or easy day's work. Perhaps the soft-focus nostalgia for some earlier time makes it *appear* that there were moments in history when teachers could somehow sharpen some pencils, close their doors, and magically meet all the needs of their students. Even if that myth was a realistic depiction of the past, we're well into an era where being an effective teacher is a complex and ever more complicated endeavor.

In this book, we explore how the work of teaching can be done so much more effectively and meaningfully when we are *in it together,* working collaboratively to help our students reach their academic potential and become active members of their learning community and beyond. We show how we can do this by drawing from the rich resources of our learning community (including teachers, students, families, the school community, and the community at large) to form a network of possibilities that can make the work of learning much more successful for all involved.

What we propose is that it is not possible for one teacher alone to meet the needs of a new era in contemporary education. Along with grappling with increasing mandates requiring that students meet specific learning standards (such as the Common Core State Standards); dramatic changes in socioeconomic, racial, cultural, and linguistic diversity among our nation's students coupled with poor outcomes and significant achievement gaps for many from these groups (commonly referred to as disproportionality); as well as budgetary constraints are affecting much of what we do. What constitutes a family is also evolving in our contemporary society—including children being raised by two parents, a single parent, blended family, grandparents, unrelated people who live cooperatively, and foster parents, and children being raised with significant support from extra familial individuals. Throughout our book, we use the terms *parent(s), parent(s)/guardian(s), and family(ies)* interchangeably to reflect the diverse family structures found within our communities. We are also living in an era when the Internet and digital technologies have radically changed our profession, from what we do in the classroom to what occurs outside of it. Authority no longer resides in a teacher's exclusive access to knowledge. Rather, it can be a keystroke or click away for students, their families, and all of us. For one thing, the omnipresence of Internet access has put instant information into everyone's hands. For another, this explosion of available information has made education a much more complex endeavor—too complex to master while working in isolation.

These dynamic changes call for a framework of teaching that allows for expertise and contributions to flow in multiple directions and from multiple sources to support all students. It requires a paradigm shift to partnerships in the learning enterprise.

Why Are Partnerships Important?

Our book is intended to provide a much-needed exploration and source for understanding how classroom, school, family, and community systems can have a powerful influence on student learning and achievement as well as on the accomplishment of school improvement goals. At the heart of our thinking is a regard for the critical importance of partnerships. What do we mean by the term *partnerships?* We use the words *partnership(s)* and *relationship(s)* interchangeably to define the positive possibilities that can and do occur when two or more people (including teachers, students, families, and members of the school community and the community at large) come together to collaborate on behalf of student learning.

Studies suggest a connection between a growing emphasis on relationships in education and powerful gains, including increased graduation rates, resources to support education, student engagement, more enduring learning, and a closer correlation of education with 21st century goals (Epstein, 2011). Throughout our book, we highlight ways in which teachers can draw on the diverse perspectives, energy, and shared interests of students, families, colleagues, and the community by cultivating relationships and inviting engagement. We also show how the cultivation of relationships in school communities has been known to cross over such important demographic differences (and often perceived barriers) as culture, ethnicity, income, education, age, and other variables and have a great influence on student outcomes. In addition, we describe how working together to connect students' personal, social, cultural, language, and world experiences to the curriculum is a powerful tool for closing the achievement gap.

Our intent is to provide a comprehensive approach for building coalitions of support around student learning and engagement through interconnected classroom community-building efforts that involve teachers: (1) building strong relationships with students, (2) intentionally supporting students to build powerful relationships with their peers, (3) fostering strong reciprocal relationships with families, (4) building relationships with the school and community at large, and (5) empowering and creating purposeful intentional spaces for everyone to deepen their relationships with each other in support of student learning.

A special feature of our book is its case study format whereby we use many examples from across the United States and Canada in K–12 settings to illustrate the concepts. In one of these, we will meet Kristina Labadie, a fourth-grade classroom teacher from the state of Washington. Kristina sought a way to provide her students with a higher volume of academic interactions and partnerships with caring adults in the community. We will also meet Maureen Penko, a speech and language pathologist from Winnipeg, Manitoba, Canada, who works in partnership with teachers, students, and families to help children on the autism spectrum to develop and strengthen their social communication skills in the classroom setting and in nonstructured situations using as many functional environments as possible.

In addition, we also provide written reflection spaces within the body of each chapter for readers to reflect on the ideas that we present directly after reading them. These are meant to delve deeper in the ideas presented and, in most cases, connect them to a personal, social, cultural, or world experience. The reflection spaces are also intended for two types of audiences: (1) an individual reader and (2) a group of readers, including professional learning communities, book groups, and students in a college classroom. Thus, you can read the book on your own and write responses in the space provided, and you can read the book with others and write responses with the intent of having a group reflection discussion about it. In addition, we include *A Closer Look* features in some of the chapters to reflect the thought process of teachers as they build a community around a classroom. Each chapter generally opens with an authentic scenario from a classroom context and focuses on key elements for creating partnerships that work. Our intent is to provide a much-needed resource for teacher educators as they work with pre- and in-service teachers, professional developers as they seek new ways of improving student outcomes, coaches as they work with teachers, and teachers to strengthen their practice. Each of the following chapter descriptions is intended for these audiences.

In Chapter 2, "An Involved Classroom Community," we introduce our sphere of influence framework for teacher-student, student-student, teacher-family, family-family, teacher–school community, and school community–community-at-large partnerships to more successfully meet the diverse needs of an ever-changing student and family population to support students' investment in learning and engagement in their learning community and beyond.

Chapter 3, "Infusing the Assets of Students and Families Into Classroom Learning," is devoted to seeing the cultural, linguistic, and personal assets of students and families as resources for the sociocultural, language/literacy, academic, and thinking-skills development of our students. We draw from Gonzalez, Moll, and Amanti (2005) to take a closer look at the rich *funds of knowledge* of students and families. We also present three research-based principles about the importance of making connections; keeping students' stress levels low; and valuing our student, family, and community assets within and beyond the classroom.

In Chapter 4, "Preparing for Classroom Community," we lay the foundation for partnerships by providing ways to develop a preliminary communication strategy for teacher-student, student-student, teacher-family, family-family, teacher-school, and school–community-at-large building efforts. We describe ways to prepare avenues of communication that include beginning-of-the-year communication, interpersonal contact, and the creation of an online presence as well as a welcoming orientation to partnership-building efforts across each of these interactive spaces.

Chapter 5, "The Academic Learning Benefits of Being 'In It Together,'" focuses on the curriculum. We provide an in-depth discussion of how to use each sphere of interaction to support student learning and give several examples of each sphere in practice.

Chapter 6, "Using Classroom Events to Empower Students and Families," presents the importance of community-building events for social purposes, showcasing the curriculum for making learning transparent, drawing on the rich resources of families, and building a home-school shared culture of learning.

In Chapter 7, "Widening the Circle Beyond the Classroom: Service Learning," we discuss the critical importance of service learning in education. We discuss how it provides students with an essential interactive space to express what they are learning and to be apprenticed supportively into being contributory citizens.

In Chapter 8, "Using Learning Partnerships in Professional Development: Applying the Ideas," we discuss how our book can be used for professional growth purposes, including book study, professional learning communities, college study, and other initiatives intended for this purpose. We provide observational, interview, survey, and reflection tasks that are intended for individual and/or collaborative use for reading the book and applying the concepts.

Why Empowerment May Be Essential to Person and Group Success

Drawing on more than 50 years of research from the behavioral sciences, Daniel Pink (2009) cogently describes what drives the kind of activity that is involved in creating the type of partnerships that we are promoting. It requires motivation and engagement, or what he calls *drive* to support it to occur. Wisely, he does not confine the drive that is needed to any one person (e.g., teacher, student); rather, it applies to all that is human and includes

- having a voice in what we do with a degree of choice and autonomy to make decisions,

- constantly striving to improve what we do and getting accurate feedback about our progress, and
- being part of something that is meaningful.

If the goal of public education is to help maintain a citizenry of informed, confident, capable, cooperative people, we have to create institutions in which all participants contribute to practice and use the skills of expression, negotiation, authority, and cooperation. This means that everyone from preschoolers to administrators practices these skills. To paraphrase Carl Jung, "We are what we do, not what we say." The first principle, having a voice, is critical. In education, our practice must show our respect for the values we want to transmit to young people. If we want them to care, the process of teaching must have care. If we want them to be open, inclusive, and respectful, we must be committed to showing these same qualities in all aspects of what we do because we are the models of what we would have them become. We also have to embrace the totality of a child's experience between and among school, home, and the community and draw from the various participants to make education work. But just as important, if we want to improve education, we must show how vital improvements are to our own practice and celebrate our successes in making these improvements. These tenets hold true for what we wish for our students—to strive to strengthen what they do to learn and to celebrate their efforts. Finally, motivation requires that we all see purpose and meaning in what we are doing so that we and our students can commit to our work whole-heartedly. Our book is based on these three interdependent elements to create and deliver the type of partnerships that are needed.

In the next chapter, we discuss the urgency for this work and the type of partnerships that support equity, access, and engagement for a diverse learning community. We also outline our framework or the spheres of influence that operate across each and every aspect of it.

References

Comer, J. (2004). *Leave no child behind: Preparing today's youth for tomorrow's world.* New Haven, CT: Yale University Press.

Epstein, J. (2011). *School, family, and community partnerships: Preparing educators and improving schools* (2nd ed.). Philadelphia, PA: Westview Press.

Gonzalez, N., Moll, L. C., & Amanti, C. (Eds.). (2005). *Funds of knowledge: Theorizing practices in households, communities, and classrooms.* Mahwah, NJ: Lawrence Erlbaum.

Pink, D. H. (2009). *Drive: The surprising truth about what motivates us.* New York, NY: Penguin Books.

2

An Involved Classroom Community

There can be no keener revelation of a society's soul than the way in which it treats its children.

—Nelson Mandela

In what ways is a teacher's vision of community vital to the success of a classroom?

While there are many opinions about public education, there is one that we can all agree on: We want all students to feel and be successful. For well over a decade, success has been shaped by federal and state accountability standards. These tell all of us—students, parents, educators as well as our local, state, and federal agencies—what it is that we expect our students to know and be able to do in order to be successful in school. We've grown so familiar with terms such as *standards-based, outcomes driven, annual state-assessments,* and *adequate yearly progress* or *AYP* that these educational terms have been woven into our profession's everyday conversations. For some groups of students, the standards are working well. For others, they have resulted in a continuous state of crisis. Unfortunately, these outcomes consistently show that school is working only for some and not for all of our students. Figure 2.1 provides a snapshot of U.S. graduation rates from 2011–2012. In it, we see the significant disparity between groups of students.

Here is one way to think about the dilemma: Imagine being a student trying to successfully meet curriculum expectations and performance standards on assessments. Now, some of us might not be too concerned, knowing that we did well in school and are not too worried about taking tests. Indeed, some of us might relish the chance to tackle an assessment! Our competitive spirit might even propel us to think that not only could we learn the standards and meet expectations, but we could possibly master them to the greatest extent possible. On the other hand, others among us may have completely different reactions, especially those of us who have struggled in school and/or think that dropping out might be our best solution. What should be done for those of us who are actually discouraged and less able to learn under the pressures of high-stakes assessment and external pressure?

A common solution for students who struggle to learn involves devoting more time to remedial skill development (what some refer to as teaching to the test) and/or additional school (also known as extending the school day). Some afterschool, summer school, year-round school, and test preparation courses typically employ these

Figure 2.1   U.S. Graduation Rates 2011–2012

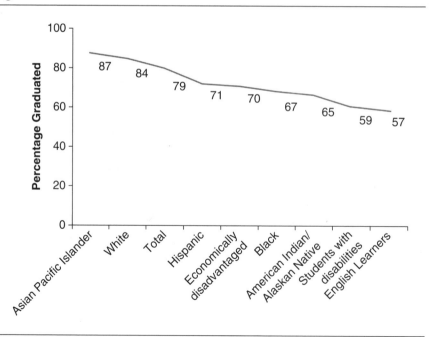

Source: U.S. Department of Education (2014).

practices. Also prevalent is the idea that class size matters and should be kept as small as possible because studies suggest that at the elementary level, at least, smaller classes have led to more effective teaching and learning (Public Schools of North Carolina, 2000). While we know that these remedies are well intentioned, they are not having the lasting effects that are intended.

For some students, these remedies have resulted in a sustained cycle of too much pressure, additional programming, separation from their classroom communities, and, most important, not enough of two critical elements:

1. active learning (also known as "learning by doing")

2. emotional engagement (caring and being cared about)

The Critical Importance of Building Partnerships

Clearly, something new is called for in education. Believe us when we say that the following example was not the first place that we expected to look. However, we think you will agree with us that the example is powerful. When Massachusetts State Trooper Michael Cutone returned to the United States in 2009 from a tour of duty as a Green Beret in Iraq, he began working in law enforcement in the particularly embattled area of Brightwood, a section in the city of Springfield, Massachusetts—an area beset with seemingly intractable crime and violence. Springfield—the birthplace of basketball, the *Merriam-Webster Dictionary*, early horseless carriages, and the Springfield Rifle—has suffered a severe economic decline (lasting more than 40 years and counting) due to the loss of manufacturing jobs that had been plentiful when it was a more thriving city.

In Brightwood, conditions had grown particularly harsh, as it had become afflicted with high crime rates and shrinking municipal services. It was also besieged with drug trafficking, gang violence, and the reputation of having the lowest priced heroin in the United States. According to Cutone, when he first came to the area, crime was so endemic that thieves would go into stores and gas stations, take what they wanted, and no one would call the police. To make things worse, drug dealers and gangs operated in the open and ordinary citizens were mainly concerned with staying out of their way.

Cutone noted that the neighborhood fit the profile of a failed state or a war zone, conditions he was familiar with from his recent military experiences. It made sense to Cutone to use the successful strategies that his unit had employed in Iraq. These involved gathering information through building relationships and winning over the general population and community leaders by (of all things) caring about their problems *and* offering help. He believed that these community-building relational efforts could work in Springfield just as well as they had in Iraq.

He mapped out an action plan which involved maximizing personal contact between the police and the people of the community by walking on streets, knocking on doors, holding town meetings with residents, and meeting with business leaders and prominent members of the community, such as politicians, health and housing representatives, and educators. His mission was to facilitate their work together to address the crime problems in the community. Creating collaborative and comprehensive partnerships with them, he believed, would greatly contribute to combating crime. Why?

These multiple partnership-building efforts created opportunities for dialogue and communication which helped the stakeholders in the community address problems too large for any one of them, especially the police, to solve on their own. The results of the efforts were dramatic and statistically measurable. According to police figures, since the initiative began, violent crime dropped by 25% and drug offenses by 50% (CBS News, 2013). Secondary benefits included a reduction in litter, graffiti, and the incidence of sexually transmitted diseases, and an increase in school attendance. As Cutone explained in an interview on the program *60 Minutes* (CBS News, 2013), building powerful partnerships with the community and enlisting its support for a shared goal made it possible to do something that would have been otherwise impossible. When critics questioned whether it was appropriate for police to take on functions that more naturally belonged with government and social service agencies, Cutone's answer is one that merits the attention of those of us who remain unconvinced or when a colleague says, "But this is the way we've always done it." Cutone's response: "Why can't the police partner with the community? The status quo of policing, it just ain't gonna work."

The Status Quo in Education "Just Ain't Gonna Work" Either

State Trooper Cutone knew what was most crucial: to build community trust by building partnerships. In addition, he understood that the types of partnerships that were needed would not occur by exercising power *over* people. Rather, these critical relationships required working in partnership *with* people. As such, he fostered a dialogue and partnerships with the community. He did this by going door to door and walking through the neighborhood to get to know its people. He also did one more thing; he called together a broad range of community members to solve problems and share perspectives about the crimes that were occurring in the neighborhood. Using this information, he mapped the community's social relationships to more effectively meet the challenges of his role as a professional.

Similar to Cutone's belief in partnerships, we believe that the job of teaching can only occur successfully through building partnerships that draw on the resources within and beyond the classroom—notably, teachers, students, family, the school community, and the community at large. Fostering partnerships is essential to the success of our students. Let's take a closer look at these possibilities by reflecting on them.

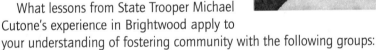

REFLECTION ACTIVITIES
Time for Reflection

Reflect on the following question and write a response.

What lessons from State Trooper Michael Cutone's experience in Brightwood apply to your understanding of fostering community with the following groups:

1. With students:

2. With families:

3. With colleagues in a school:

(Continued)

(Continued)

How might you apply Cutone's experience to a classroom for one of the following three reasons: (1) to increase family attendance at classroom events, (2) to develop students' homework habits, or (3) to address chronic absenteeism. Describe the purpose of these activities.

If you were convening a meeting of school community members to support your efforts, who would you be sure to include, and why?

Understanding Interconnected Spheres of Influence

Figure 2.2 illustrates the type of mapping that is helpful in understanding the social relationships that build a school community. It is based on our core belief that students learn best when it is demonstrated to them that their peers, teachers, family members, school community, and community at large respect and care about them and are curious to know more about them above and beyond their role as learners. This allows students to better trust and share information with adults and peers as an emotional foundation for learning and cooperation, which ultimately enhances learning outcomes. In addition, students learn best when their classrooms are conceptualized around caring, trusting interconnected

Figure 2.2   Building Community Around a Classroom: Spheres of Influence

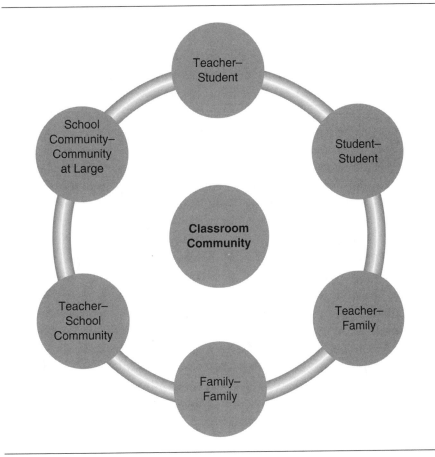

spheres of influence: students, families, the school community, and the community at large. We believe that these groups should not be separate, because when they work together, the possibilities for student growth and potential, socially and academically, can rise exponentially. As such, we call them *spheres of influence* to reflect their relational aspect.

Connection Between the Spheres of Influence and Improving Education

James Gee (2009), a renowned sociolinguist and psycholinguist, points to the importance of understanding literacy as a shared, collaborative, social, and cultural achievement. An important concept in exploring these spheres of influence is their connection to the promotion of knowledge and the cultivation of skills needed to participate in a democratic society (Alexander & Alexander, 2012; Shields, 2011).

Curriculum standards, such as the Common Core State Standards, outline the knowledge and academic skills that have been determined to be essential for student achievement. However, they are not primarily oriented toward the equally urgent goal of creating communities of civil cooperation and collaboration. That is, they do not provide us with the means/methods to apprentice students into the practices of learning, socializing, and working with each other. Creating spaces for these purposes serves the essential function of empowering students to exercise their own agency as *active* learners and *citizens* of their learning communities and beyond.

What is equally vital to this work is an understanding that our student population has changed dramatically and is continuing to do so in ways that make the creation of community a more complex endeavor. Rural, suburban, and urban districts have become and are becoming more and more racially, culturally, ethnically, economically, and linguistically diverse and are reflective of what has become an ever more *global culture.* Along with helping all of our students pass state-mandated assessments and meet accountability standards, we have to be equally committed to creating democratic and culturally responsive classroom communities that honor the diverse personal, cultural, social, and world experiences of our student and family populations.

The social ingredient to learning—the relationships of emotional connection that go far beyond having behaviors controlled or coerced or even incentivized—is what infuses learning communities with resilience and commitment. If we liken effective education to the art of baking, relationships represent the essential binding ingredient— the eggs, the butter that is the difference between a savory confection and a crumbly bowl of high quality ingredients.

Promoting partnerships is more important and urgent than ever if we hope to promote a civil society that is founded on mutual respect and caring. Building partnerships with students and among students should be a core tenet of every classroom. The fostering of community in public schools ultimately represents the cultivation of citizens who are responsible to each other and to the larger society that they share. That in and of itself is a worthy goal, but it also is a practical one. Members of a learning community learn more effectively.

The Importance of Teacher-Student Partnerships

John Hattie (2008) completed the largest meta-analysis of educational research of the key factors that affect student achievement. Of the 138 influences and effects that he studied, teacher-student relationships as well as feedback ranked among the top 8%. Looking more closely at his findings reveals that *trusting* relationships are key for this to occur successfully. Because so many of us do not represent the racial, cultural, economic, and language backgrounds of our students, we have to think more proactively about what we can do to ensure that the partnerships that we forge with students are meaningful and empowering for them. As we will discuss throughout this book, this type of relationship building relies heavily on our empathetic understanding of students' personal, cultural, linguistic, socioeconomic, as well as world experiences and building a learning community based on this understanding.

The Importance of the Student-Student Sphere of Influence

Hattie's findings also reveal that collaborative (peer-peer) learning ranks among the top 17% in terms of its influence and effect on student learning. While this is highly important for us to consider, so is the need to understand the changes that are occurring in our nation's population. We are becoming much more racially diverse, as seen in Figure 2.3. In addition, the population of English learners in our nation's schools has been steadily increasing for over a decade (National Center for Education Statistics, 2013). These shifts should raise our level of urgency to better understand the diverse identities, beliefs, and practices of our students.

While all students experience differences between their home and school cultures, these are much more pronounced for some minority students, and this greatly impacts their academic performance (Gay, 2005; Tyler et al., 2008). Research on public school practices shows a difference between a mainstream cultural belief in individualism and competition versus a minority belief in collectivism. Individualistic cultures, including dominant U.S. culture, lean toward minimizing student interaction, preferring a controlled quiet classroom, expecting students to learn by themselves, and favoring independence and competition (American Psychological Association, 2003; Tyler et al., 2008). These cultural values and beliefs differ from those who favor a collectivist system of interdependence and interconnectedness. While each minority group has its own way of being and acting, this fundamental belief in collectivism has been found across all underrepresented groups (Tyler et al., 2008). One of the urgent reasons for paying much more attention to a preference for peer-peer interactions goes beyond the research that shows it to be an important method for all students (Cohen & Lotan, 2003). Peer-peer interactions are also a much closer cultural match for students across all underrepresented populations.

Figure 2.3   Nation's Growth Patterns 2000–2010

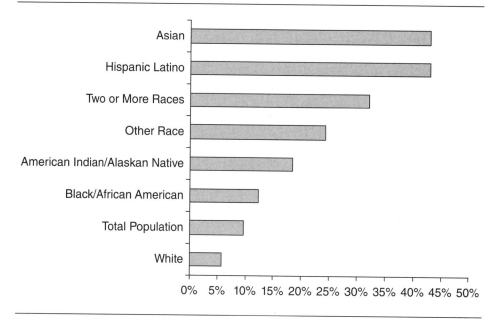

Source: Humes, Jones, & Ramirez (2010).

Fostering a positive social-emotional climate between and among students is encouraging, as is fostering children's curiosity and interests about their peers. Jennifer Melton is a teacher of English to speakers of other languages (ESOL) at Hardeeville Elementary School (HES), in Hardeeville, South Carolina. She highlights some of the complexities that occur when students are separated. In her school, some English learners leave their grade-level classrooms to receive instruction in ESOL. Jennifer found that English-fluent students wanted to come to their peers' classes and arranged for them to attend an ESOL class at the end of each school year. As we will see, they wanted to come earlier and frequently asked Jennifer how soon they could come.

 **A CLOSER LOOK**
Jennifer Melton

A second-grade general education student asked, "When can we go back to ESOL? Can we go today?" As the ESOL teacher, I answered, "You can come in the fourth quarter. Remember, after all of the tests are over." "Does that mean we go tomorrow or next week?" "No, wait until May, fourth quarter" is my general response.

On average, a conversation similar to this happens at least once a week. The students have such a curiosity about this illusive place called ESOL. "What is there? What is it like? Why do some kids get to go and not others? I want to go back. I enjoy the activities and treats that accompany the ESOL class." These are some of the interactions that occur in the minds of general education students.

As curious as the students have been, there has also been some misunderstanding about this wonderful class where students look so excited at their chance to attend. On more than one occasion, a few first-grade students have openly asked, "Why do you only take the Spanish kids? What don't you take the other kids?" It is heartbreaking to hear those questions, because they can view it as an opportunity lost. I respond, "You have to know two languages." Sometimes students will say that they know two languages, and they will respond with the few Spanish words that they can recall.

Jennifer works in a school that is quite diverse. Using data from her school, she reported that "the student population is 51% African American, 33% Latino, 15% Caucasian, and 1% Asian." Jennifer sought a solution that would support the goal of bringing students together. In her own words, she describes two types of ESOL classes that she teaches: *pullout,* when students leave their general education classes to work with her, and *push-in,* when she goes in to general education classes to work with her students. She states that both have the potential to be problematic without her attending to the larger goal of supporting students to learn and work together:

There is a need for cultural awareness and student cooperation. Otherwise, there is a possibility for student conflict to occur in future years. Potentially, ESOL pullouts and push-ins can become points of contention that overshadow actual intervention benefits. Therefore, it is important that this interaction with ESOL happens on a grand scale to support cultural awareness.

She describes her efforts to bring the groups of students together:

Throughout the last few weeks of school, first- and second-grade general education students are able to learn alongside their ESOL friends. The English learners and general education students participate jointly in peer groups, computer activities, phonics activities, reader's theater, and/or musical content-related endeavors.

Jennifer discusses the successes that occur when general education students attend classes designed exclusively for English learners. She also asks some important questions about what might have been missed had this opportunity not been provided.

The general education students appreciate the attention and recognition. The ESOL students enjoy the chance to share their ESOL class and culture. The general education students are amazed to find lessons with grammar and vocabulary. Each time they comment that they are surprised to hear languages such as Spanish and Chinese used to acquire new academic concepts. The general education and ESOL students react as though they know more because of the cooperative learning.

If this end-of-the-year opportunity did not occur, the understanding and excitement for cooperation might diminish. For instance, because of this collaboration, the second graders do not ask about which students attend and why. Through their ESOL class participation, they are fully aware of the aspect of two languages and what it entails. Also, there is less division among the groups of students that can continue throughout the grades and classes.

The enthusiasm for learning in ESOL should not decrease for some versus others. Students should be able to support one another in their pursuit of an education. Education is not meant to be an exclusionary or elitist venture. We are Americans who learn in group settings, and our students are no different. They should be provided with the ability to share, interact, and learn together in a variety of settings, including the occasional ESOL classroom at the end of the year. Then we can all eagerly await the reward of a day in an ESOL classroom, just like many students at HES.

REFLECTION ACTIVITIES

Time for Reflection

Reflect on the following and write a response.

In your work setting, or in K–12 schools you know best, do general education students interact in the physical spaces/classrooms allocated for students with special education needs; students receiving Title 1, reading, or mathematics support; or students who are English learners and receive bilingual or English language development instruction?

☐ Yes
☐ No

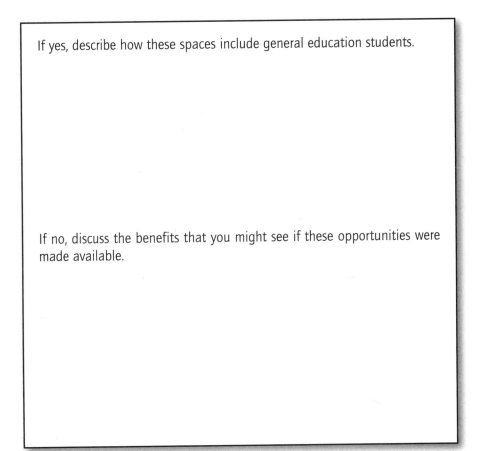

If yes, describe how these spaces include general education students.

If no, discuss the benefits that you might see if these opportunities were made available.

Along with supporting students to work together, our partnership framework looks closely at working with families. This is especially critical as we consider the disparate outcomes among our students.

The Crucial Importance of Family Involvement

Increasing rates of students and families living in significant poverty (National Center for Education Statistics, 2014) and chronic school absenteeism among the nation's poor (Balfanz & Byrnes, 2012) have renewed our nation's interest in creating more effective educational programming. Coupled with the persistent challenge of significant dropout rates, particularly among Latino, Black, and American Indian students (Swanson, 2011), this raises a good deal of concern about U.S. schools. The growing population of English learners (National Center for Education Statistics, 2013) is also propelling the urgency to find more effective means for educating the nation's public and public charter school students. While creating standards, such as the Common Core State Standards, is an important step in helping educators come to agreement about what it is we expect students to know and be able to do, there is need for greater emphasis on enhancing the cooperative participation of students, teachers, families, the school community, and the community at large in the great work of educating the nation's students. We must do this for a number of important reasons.

In theory, we understand the significance of family-school engagement. That is, as educators, we expect that this will occur to some degree. We hold a number of activities and events for this purpose. Parent-teacher conferences, Open House, school plays and other performance-based events, and parent council meetings are standard and conventional activities that occur in our nation's schools (Zacarian, 2011; Zacarian & Haynes, 2012). In fact, as you read that list of activities, it's likely that you had an image of each one and could describe it in detail. In this respect, schools maintain consistency nationwide, like store chains such as Home Depot. Whether we are in Florida or California, the Home Depot sign is the same and the store's physical layout (in terms of electrical, appliance, plumbing, garden, and other items for sale) appears to be the same (probably intentionally).

Research on teachers' attitudes about parent involvement, however, shows that there are marked differences in the degree of parent involvement that teachers expect outside of these highly controlled and teacher-managed occasions. (Henderson, Mapp, Johnson, & Davies, 2007). Epstein's (1986) seminal and frequently cited research study on parents' attitudes about their child's school provides us with important insights on this topic and is punctuated by more recent work in this area. In this study, parents from a range of educational experiences, including those with no high school diploma to those with graduate degrees, reported that they felt positively about their child's school and believed it was well run. However, they also believed the following:

- Teachers could do more to involve parents.
- The relationship between teachers and parents was too information-driven.
- Parents did not feel as able to help older children with school work as they did with younger children.
- Teachers could do more to show parents how they might help their child in school. (Epstein, 1986)

While these findings are very important for us to consider as we build partnerships with parents, perhaps the most fundamental reason for family-school engagement is the influence that school and family systems have on a child's development (Bartle-Haring, Younkin, & Day, 2012). It can carry a message that our students can be empowered to be active learners and members of their school community. We might not be thinking of this in terms of the interconnectedness between the two environments in which children interact, and we should. In addition, we should consider the reality that our students spend more time, literally, out of school than they do in it and that our partnerships with families is critical to students' success.

Recognizing the Challenges of Preparation and Preferences in Building Teacher-Family Partnerships

To recognize family partnerships as an important goal, we also have to recognize some of our limitations in implementing them effectively, as a profession. First, most teacher education programs do not provide training in this important area (Caspe, Lopez, Chu, & Weiss, 2011). We tend to learn about working with parents based on our assumptions about an educator's role, from our peers and others, and on the job. This learn-as-we-go method of operation leaves much to chance and circumstance.

Equally complicating factors are that our schools are becoming more and more socioeconomically, racially, culturally, and linguistically diverse and many families have much less education and fewer resources available to them than we do (Hollins & Guzman, 2005). We also do not have much experience working with people unlike ourselves (Hollins & Guzman, 2005). How many of us in the teaching ranks, for example, grew up living in poverty? In addition, many who teach in poor urban and rural areas with people of color were "fast-tracked" into teaching in these communities without the level of adequate training and preparation that we need (Zeichner, 2012). This does not mean that we cannot learn how to effectively work with families living in poverty and others who represent socioeconomic, racial, cultural, and linguistic groups that are distinct from our own. In fact, our core argument is that it is a must and that the benefits for our students can increase dramatically when we organize our classroom community for this type of active and engaged participation and engagement.

To do this, we have to consider the various communities that our majority and minority students participate in (family, school, community, etc.) and think carefully about the types of partnerships that we are building to foster the interconnections that are possible among them. We also have to consider the activities that the majority of our students are involved in and the minority are not (such as town/city sports, Girl and Boy Scouts, etc.). Why? Our students do not live in a vacuum. Their world experience in and out of school is an essential factor of learning. It is critical that families and schools communicate closely together about the challenges and successes that students face in school and home and build partnerships to mutually support students' development.

REFLECTION ACTIVITIES
Time for Reflection

Reflect on the following and write a response.
    Describe two ways in which you see the parent and school systems as interconnected.

1.

2.

Consider the ways in which your parents were involved in your education as an elementary, middle, and high school student. Did you notice a drop-off in involvement as you came of age? What might have been the advantages and disadvantages in these involvement shifts?

Understanding the Family-Family Sphere of Influence

While school-family partnerships are critical, it is helpful for us to take stock of who is involved and who isn't. The goal of this type of review is to explore the idea of partnerships from a variety of perspectives and form a well-grounded idea of the concept in our own particular settings. Also, as much as we expect schools to promote the tenets of a democracy, it does not happen in isolation and may not be easily realized among our students' family communities.

Some families may feel that they are not welcome, have no voice, and/or are rejected by other families (Henderson et al., 2007; Zacarian, 2011, 2013; Zacarian & Haynes, 2012). An equally complicating factor is that some families may perceive that they should not be involved in their child's school as it is not their role to do so. While these are complex factors, it is highly worth the effort to take steps to support families' involvement with each other. Families are a great source of support, cooperation, and collaboration. These partnerships can increase when we support them. To do this well requires that we look more closely at issues of equity as it applies to race, socioeconomic, as well as linguistic and cultural differences.

One area of importance around equity issues may be the differences between dominant U.S. culture, which favors individualism and competition, and the growth in family populations who represent collectivist cultures. The following is a small hypothetical example of the two cultures at play.

A school is attempting to raise money for field trips by having a bake sale. Individuals from dominant U.S. culture bake items on their own, hoping that what they bake will be the top-selling items. Groups from collectivist cultures gather together to bake the items and join in selling them at the sale. For the families from collectivist cultures, the communicative social *process* of the activity is of import, whereas for people from the dominant U.S. culture the *products* (the baked goods) are.

What is key for us is to challenge ourselves to look closely at the ways in which we create activities that are both collaborative and social. Take, for example, the ways in which parents are oriented to their child's school. In some schools, this occurs in the sole form of completing a variety of enrollment forms (Zacarian, 2011). If we are to examine this process, we see that it lacks a collaborative or social arena. Henderson et al. (2007) remind us of the importance of families working together through such events as a 6-week enrollment program to help facilitate families' entry into becoming and then being active members of their school communities. Along with introducing the goals and objectives of school and learning, their value in bringing groups together to work and socialize is critical.

REFLECTION ACTIVITIES
Time for Reflection

Reflect on the following and write a response.
   Provide two or three activity examples of how families from different racial, socioeconomic, linguistic, and cultural backgrounds can collaborate and work together. Include the goals for these activities.

1.

2.

3.

How will the activities that you created take into account families who do not speak in English?

What do you see as the challenges of these activities, and how would you address them? Provide one or two examples.

Understanding Teachers and the School Community as Interconnected Spheres of Influence

As with family-school partnerships, the importance of a teacher's partnership with his or her school community is also a central component. We have to remember that we are not alone in our quest for students to be successful. Accessing and engaging support is powerful for many reasons. One of the key reasons is that it sends a message to students and their families that their membership in the school community extends beyond the classroom. It also spans the years and grade levels by a team of educators who unconditionally know and care about them.

Understanding the School Community and the Community at Large as an Essential Interconnected Sphere of Influence

While we might believe in the relationship between our school communities and the community at large, we may feel that there is no time for this type of activity or that it is the responsibility of someone else such as the school principal, guidance counselor, or outreach worker. It should be part of the core of what we all do because it represents the types of interconnections and, most important, interactions that we believe to be at the heart of what matters. The following is an example of this sphere of influence in action. As you read it, consider possibilities for collaboration among teacher, students, families, a school community, and the community at large.

A CLOSER LOOK
The School Community and the Community at Large

A group of non-English-speaking refugees enrolled in an elementary school in a large suburban district. By the time they entered the district's middle school, they had become fluent in English and no longer received bilingual support or instruction in English as a second language (ESL). When they enrolled in high school, they often skipped school. One day, the high school's ESL teacher was asked by one of the biology teachers why the group was skipping. Though she did not know the students, she discovered that they were coming to school for breakfast and lunch and walking out of the school after these meals.

She contacted the district's director of bilingual programming for help. The director contacted the students' families and their prior elementary and middle school ESL, bilingual, and classroom teachers. They suggested contacting certain members of the students' community, including key leaders and other family members from their faith-based communities. Members from these groups suggested that a meeting of families, faith-based leaders, elementary, middle, and high school staff, administrators, and central office staff be convened.

Like State Trooper Michael Cutone did with crime prevention, when they convened, they mapped a plan for keeping the students in school. One of the activities was for the former elementary teachers to come to the high school for breakfast and lunch with the students as they had strong and trusting relationships with the students. Another was to adjust the students' schedules so that the first period of school involved supporting them as mentors for new English learners. The teachers, administrators, and community members also worked with the students' high school teachers to build trusting relationships with the students and use a collaborative peer-peer method of teaching. Simultaneously, the school worked closely with the family, school, and community at large. Within a short period of time, all of the students returned to school. They later passed the state English language arts and mathematics tests, graduated, and went to college. Many of the students commented that the reason they stayed and were successful in school was because of the care and support they received from these various communities.

Summary

In this chapter, we discussed the rapid demographic shifts that are occurring among the nation's population and the disparate outcomes for students from some underrepresented groups. We introduced our sphere-of-influence framework and the urgent need for teacher-student, student-student, teacher-family, family-family, teacher–school community, and school community–community-at-large partnerships to more successfully meet the needs of our dynamically changing student and family populations.

In the next chapter, we take a closer look at the cultural, linguistic, and personal assets of students and families and present research-based principles about the importance of making connections, keeping students' stress levels low, and valuing the assets and resources within and beyond our classrooms.

References

Alexander, K., & Alexander, M. D. (2012). *American public school law* (8th ed.). Independence, KY: Cengage.

American Psychological Association. (2003). Guidelines on multicultural education, training, research, practice, and organizational change for psychologists. *American Psychologist, 58,* 377–402. doi:10.1037/0003-066X.58.5.377

Balfanz, R., & Byrnes, V. (2012). *Chronic absenteeism: Summarizing what we know from nationally available data.* Baltimore, MD: Johns Hopkins University, Center for Social Organization of Schools.

Bartle-Haring, S., Younkin, F. L., & Day, R. (2012). Family distance regulation and school engagement in middle-school-aged children. *Family Relations, 61,* 192–206. doi:10.1111/j.1741-3729.2011.00698.x

Caspe, M., Lopez, M. E., Chu, A., & Weiss, B. (2011). *Teaching the teachers: Preparing educators to engage families for student achievement.* Harvard Family Research Project Issue Brief. Retrieved from: http://www.metrostatecue.org/files/mscd//Documents/Community%20Overview/Harvard%20Family%20Research%20Project_Teaching%20the%20Teachers.pdf

CBS News. (2013, May 5). Counterinsurgency cops: Military tactics fight street crime. *60 Minutes.* Retrieved from http://www.cbsnews.com

Cohen, E. G., & Lotan, R. A. (2003). Equity in heterogeneous classrooms. In J. Banks & C. Banks (Eds.), *Handbook of multicultural education* (2nd ed.). New York, NY: Teachers College Press.

Epstein, J. (1986). Parents' reaction to teacher practices of parent involvement. *Elementary School Journal, 86,* 277–294.

Gay, G. (2005). Politics of multicultural teacher education. *Journal of Teacher Education, 56,* 221–229. doi:10.1177/0022487105275913

Gee, J. P. (2009). *A situated sociocultural approach to literacy and technology.* Arizona State University. Retrieved from http://www.jamespaulgee.com/sites/default/files/pub/Approach%20to%20Literacy%20Paper.pdf

Hattie, J. A. (2008). *Visible learning: A synthesis of over 800 meta-analyses relating to achievement.* New York, NY: Routledge.

Henderson, A. T., Mapp, K. L., Johnson, V. R., & Davies, D. (2007). *Beyond the bake sale: The essential guide to family-school partnerships.* New York, NY: New Press.

Hollins, E., & Guzman, M. T. (2005). Research on preparing teachers for diverse populations. In M. Cochran & K. M. Zeichner (Eds.), *Studying teacher education: The report of the AERA Parent on Research and Teacher Education* (pp. 477–548). Mahwah, NJ: Lawrence Erlbaum.

Humes, K. R., Jones, N. A., & Ramirez, R. R. (2010). *Overview of race and Hispanic origin: 2010.* Retrieved from http://www.census.gov/prod/cen2010/briefs/c2010br-02.pdf

Lawrence-Lightfoot, S. (2003). *The essential conversation: What parents and teachers can learn from each other.* New York, NY: Random House.

National Center for Education Statistics. (2013). *Table 204.20: Number and percentage of public school students participating in programs for English language learners, by state: Selected years, 2002–03 through 2011–12.* Retrieved from http://nces.ed.gov/programs/digest/d13/tables/dt13_204.20.asp

National Center for Education Statistics. (2014). *Concentration of public school students eligible for free or reduced-price lunch.* Retrieved from http://nces.ed.gov/programs/coe/indicator_clb.asp

Public Schools of North Carolina. (2000). *School size and its relationship with achievement and behavior.* Retrieved from http://www.ncpublicschools.org/docs/data/reports/size.pdf

Shields, D. L. (2011). Character as the aim of education. *Phi Delta Kappan, 92*(8), 48–53. doi:10.1177/003172171109200810

Swanson, C. (2011). Nation turns a corner. *Diplomas count 2011: Beyond high school: Before baccalaureate.* Retrieved from http://www.edweek.org/ew/toc/2011/06/09/index.html

Tyler, K. M., Uqdah, A. L., Dillihunt, M. L., Beatty-Hazelbaker, R., Conner, T., Gadson, N., . . . Stevens, R. (2008). Cultural discontinuity: Toward a quantitative investigation of a major hypothesis in education. *Educational Researcher, 37*, 280–297. doi:10.3102/0013189X08321459

U.S. Department of Education. (2014). *Public high school four-year on-time graduation rates and event dropout rates: School years 2010–11 and 2011–12.* Retrieved from http://nces.ed.gov/pubs2014/2014391.pdf

Zacarian, D. (2011). *Transforming schools for English learners: A comprehensive framework for school leaders.* Thousand Oaks, CA: Corwin.

Zacarian, D. (2013). *Mastering academic language: A framework for supporting student achievement.* Thousand Oaks, CA: Corwin.

Zacarian, D., & Haynes, J. (2012). *The essential guide for educating beginning English learners.* Thousand Oaks, CA: Corwin.

Zeichner, K. (2012). *Two visions of teaching and teacher education for the twenty-first century.* Dartmouth, MA: University of Massachusetts, Dartmouth, Centre for Policy Analysis.

3

Infusing the Assets of Students and Families Into Classroom Learning

The way schools care about children is reflected in the way schools care about the children's families.

—Joyce Epstein et al. (2009, p. 9)

> Why is it critical to conceptualize students and families as having rich personal, cultural, and linguistic assets and resources from which to build learning communities?

Ernest Conklin is a high school biology teacher in a small urban district. His class is engaged in a unit of study on mitosis and meiosis, the process by which cells separate. He has separated his class into small groups of four and is requiring each group to create a poster about one of these concepts. During the school's Curriculum Night,[1] his expectation is that parents will (1) learn about the unit of study, (2) view the posters his students created, and (3) learn about

---

[1]Open House, also known as Curriculum Night, refers to an evening when parents learn about their child's daily schedule as well as the curricular goals of particular subject matters that their child is learning.

the next unit of study. If we step back and look at Ernest's biology class and parent Curriculum Night, we see a range of behaviors.

In observing his students in their cooperative learning groups, we see some who get along well and others whose behavior ranges from polite disagreement to an all-out war of words. In addition, we see that some of his students are actively engaged in the poster-making process, some are quite passive and hardly participate at all, and we note a few empty seats that represent the students who chronically skip his class. If we look at the activities that Ernest has his students engaging in, we see that he generally provides a lecture requiring his students to listen and take notes and that he relies heavily on the tasks furnished in the course text. These include lab experiments that involve identification and labeling of cell parts, review of vocabulary terms, and short quizzes (done individually and in pairs) composed of responding to multiple-choice, fill-in-the-blank, and critical thinking questions. When we attend the Curriculum Night, we learn that Ernest considers himself lucky if 30% of his parent community attends.

These behaviors and outcomes may be all too familiar for many of us. While we want our students and their families to participate in what we do, it is challenging for us to realize this goal. Some of us might think that we should opt out of using cooperative learning groups in our classrooms because they pose so much tension in terms of classroom management of student behaviors in the *process* of this method and ensuring that each student is active in the *product* or *task* that the group is assigned. We may resort to finding ourselves lecturing more as, like many secondary teachers across the United States, we find ourselves believing that this format is a much more efficient and effective way to cover the curriculum that we are required to do (Foote et al., 2004). And upon reflection, we might find that Ernest is playing a role on Curriculum Night that is quite familiar to many of us. His script goes something like this:

> Welcome, parents. It is a pleasure to have you in my third-period biology class where we have just completed a unit of study on the life cycle of cells and reproduction from our biology book. (He holds up the biology book that his students are using.) During our class, your children have been learning about the phases of a cell's life cycle, the process of mitosis and meiosis, and the process of reproduction. During the unit, your children created these beautiful posters (points to the walls) about the process of mitosis and meiosis. Please have a look at your child's poster before you leave. Our next unit of study is on inheritance patterns in life cycles. We will be exploring the importance of chromosomes.

Like Ernest, we may find that we have not really thought of events, such as Curriculum Night, in terms of their potential for partnerships and the various resources of our classroom community. What Ernest did is what we have come to know as a conventional or traditional practice of the teacher as the authority.

The Importance of Interaction

In this chapter, we will explore an alternative to what traditionally occurs to allow for the richness and resources of our student and family communities to be tapped. We will look through the lens of our interactive framework of teacher-student, student-student, teacher-family, family-family, teacher–school community, school community–community-at-large schema. We use the term *schema* to refer to the interactive spaces that we must intentionally create. John Dewey, one of the most influential educational philosophers of the 20th century, discussed the importance of *active* participation. Rather than view students as empty vessels that their all-knowing teachers needed to fill, he directed our attention to propelling learning through the act of *doing.* Where does this occur? Interactions and many of them! In fact, Paul Nation (2001), a world-renowned educational linguist, points to the importance of multiple interactive practice opportunities as being key levers to literacy and membership in a cultural community. In the case of school, we believe that the culture in which education occurs requires us to think anew about the interactive spaces that we must create for this active type of membership to occur well for everyone. In Chapter 2, we provided a framework for these interactive spaces. In this chapter, we illustrate the type of actions (in this case *interac*tions) that are critical to include.

To illustrate what we mean by active participation in a learning community, let's go back to Ernest's Curriculum Night in which he welcomes the parents who show up to learn about their child's third-period biology class. During the event, what spaces do we see for parents to interact with Ernest and each other? They are extremely limited. Rather, this event has certain implied rules for being and acting, namely that parents will come to the event to listen passively to what their child's teacher says. In a real sense, it positions Ernest as the all-responsible, all-knowing authority of his subject matter and of their children. He marks this authority with the subject-specific language that he uses: "Your children have been learning about the phases of a cell's life cycle, the process of mitosis and meiosis, and the process of reproduction." Such a role places an unnecessary burden on him as an educator and is an unavoidable obstacle to greater parent involvement. Some of us may expect a teacher to lecture about the curriculum in just this way—it is a curriculum night, after all! We might also think that the strategy behind his comments is to tell parents not to worry, that the specialized work of learning biology may sound complicated but parents can trust him in teaching their children. Following this train of thought, we might not be thinking of this as an important opportunity for us to engage parents in the act of doing to become members of this community.

To push this point further, let's also look at Ernest's class on mitosis. As students arrive, he greets them by their first name at the door. We also observe him having small personal exchanges with many of his students. "I see the team won the basketball game last night. Good job!" he comments to one. "How was the homework for you?" he asks another. These exemplify the interest that he has in each of his students. We also note that the students' respond politely to Ernest. On the board, he has written a "ready for class" assignment that says: "Talk with your lab partner about questions that you have about last night's reading." As students file in, they engage in the task. This occurs during the first 5 minutes of class. During the next 20 minutes, Ernest provides a lecture on mitosis, the section from the course text that they have read. He enthusiastically points his students to the exact passages from their course text about this biological process. He uses specific academic language and terms and presents many examples of the process in action. During the subsequent 20 minutes, he divides the class into pairs, provides each pair with a handout of the mitosis process, and assigns them the task of labeling the handout with the biology vocabulary that he provided during the lecture. At the end of the class, he reviews what they have learned and assigns them homework to read the next section of the chapter on meiosis.

After our observation, Ernest meets with a colleague who has offered to observe with us and reflect on his teaching. He asks his colleague for her thoughts about his lesson. He does this by saying the following:

> I am looking for some ideas about how to make my lessons and my work with parents more meaningful and purposeful. I am doing this for many reasons. First, I know that many of my students are not engaged in my class and some are failing. I would welcome more participation from my student and family community. Could you give me a few suggestions that would make my lessons and work with families more effective?

He and his coaching partner brainstorm some ideas for achieving this goal. One idea is to have students prepare a poster to explain the concept to parents/guardians during Curriculum Night. Their hope is that the activity will give students autonomy to think creatively about how to make the complex content ideas simple to understand, the chance to receive feedback from Ernest and their peers so as to strengthen their understanding, and the opportunity to do something that is meaningful. Ernest and his coaching partner also hope that more parents/guardians will come to Curriculum Night to see their children's projects.

REFLECTION ACTIVITIES

Time for Reflection

Reflect on the following question and write a response.

Suggest an additional way that Ernest could raise the level of interaction between him and his students and among his students. Be creative, as he is looking for ideas that are outside the box and will transform how he teaches students whom he is struggling to reach and who are struggling to learn.

Suggest an additional way that Ernest might involve families in student learning about the concepts that he is teaching. Be creative, as he is looking for ideas that are outside the box and will transform how he works with the families.

What Involvement and Engagement of Students and Their Families Is Meaningful?

It's likely that we would have provided some concrete suggestions to help Ernest support students and families to be more actively engaged, and that's a good thing! The ideas that we created highlight our capacity to do the same for ours, using methods that are intuitive and natural to us, that are waiting for us to use in our own practice. During this segment of the chapter, we introduce some key ideas to consider. Included in our discussion are three research-based practices that support students to have a greater sense of trust and comfort with each other so that they might benefit academically from classroom learning interactions:

1. Making connections

2. Keeping students' stress levels low

3. Valuing the assets within and beyond the classroom

Making Connections

While we may intuitively know the importance of relating to all students, we also have bodies of research that point to principles of connection making. Of particular note, brain-based educational scholars suggest that the instructional practices that we build and maintain must, at a foundational level, build pathways to learning in two very important ways. First, we must build from students' past experiences to stimulate or activate learning (Jensen, 2008; Sylwester, 2010). Our students' and their families' personal, social, cultural, literacy, and world experiences can greatly help us build connections to learning (Freire, 1970; Jensen, 2008; Sylwester, 2010; Vasquez, 2014; Zacarian, 2011, 2013).

If we consider the reality that each of our students comes to us with a good deal of experiences, as do their families, we can see the opportunities for building connections between what they already know and what is to be learned. Take, for example, the process of mitosis that Ernest is teaching. The biological process is quite dependent on students having prior understanding about cells and replication. To help the students learn this process, Ernest has to ensure that each of them already knows what cells are and what the process of replication means and that he teaches these concepts to anyone who does not possess this critical knowledge. Because learning involves making meaning, he must also consider how to help his students connect to these concepts on a personal, social, cultural, linguistic, and world experience level. Some biology teachers might choose to show a film about reproduction, and others might have students create models of cells from clay to support this much-needed meaning-making. What is fundamental to whatever we do is to be sure that we are making connections with our students' various backgrounds for learning to occur meaningfully for them.

A second step is equally important here: connecting learning with students' families. As the people who have the greatest amount of experiential and emotional connection with our students, families have immense potential as a resource for learning. It is hugely beneficial to take full advantage of this. Family involvement has long been studied and known as a key factor for student success. Some families' practices mirror what is done in school (particularly families who engage in a high level of literacy practices) and some do not (Epstein et al., 2009; Zacarian, 2011, 2013). An important step that Ernest must take is to help all of his students and families see that he values and honors their experiences and draws from them to create a positive strength-based learning environment.

Let's return to the idea that he and his colleague discussed about having small groups of students prepare a poster to explain the biological concepts of mitosis and meiosis to parents/guardians that make them as easy to understand as possible using everyday language. We focus on one group of students. This group has created two posters that depict meiosis and mitosis collectively. Before Curriculum Night, Ernest asks each group to share their poster creations with another group and receive feedback about what is working and what needs strengthening in order to make it the most simple to understand. He walks around the classroom as these activities are occurring. With the group that created the two posters, he observes that each student is taking ownership of the learning that she or he has done. Diane, a student that he had previously observed as reluctant to speak in class, is proudly sharing her knowledge about the poster. He cannot wait to tell his colleague about his observations!

Following this plan, Ernest readies for Curriculum Night. He invites his students to attend the event and asks them to bring their parents/guardians. His plan is for them to share their projects with their families.

REFLECTION ACTIVITIES
Time for Reflection

Reflect on the following question and write a response.

(Continued)

(Continued)

Discuss two activities that you might do to enhance Ernest's plan to make the Curriculum Night event successful.

1.

2.

Keeping Students' Stress Levels Low

According to Sylwester (2010) and other brain-based scholars, humans use two systems of action: one reflexive and the other reflective. We use the reflexive system to quickly make decisions regarding the safety and immediacy of a problem. Some of us might be familiar with this concept as the *fight/flight response* coined in the 1920s by physiologist Walter Cannon (1927). Cannon used this term to describe how our bodies react when we perceive danger/stress. Sylwester calls this a reflexive response that represents an emotion or feeling of stress. A hypothetical example of this might be the following scenario. We failed the most recent quiz in Ernest's class. The next day, Ernest says the following as we walk into his classroom: "You are never going to pass this class." How might we react to his declaration? We might do so reflexively in two different ways. First, we might fight back by saying something reactionary. Second, we might skip his class. Hence, we fight or flee. Both of these reactions are in response to the danger/stress that we perceive. According to sociologist Claude Steele (2010), these perceptions can have particularly deleterious effects for some groups of students who perceive themselves to be in a racial, ethnic, linguistic, cultural, economic, or gender category that is not expected to show mastery skills. Because students are devoting their energy to a fight-or-flight mode, they are in a reactive state.

Sylwester (2010) suggests that our less reactionary brain, our reflective one, takes time to develop and involves our being supported in this way of thinking through a *nurtured* practice or apprenticeship into it. Let's go back to Ernest's greeting. What might be the reaction of the same failing student to the following greeting: "I am so happy to see you. Today, let's talk about how to make this class work as well as I know it can for you. Can we meet after class?" While this might not be a perfect example of what we each might say, it shows how to apply the research evidence in our work. Steele (2010) talks about an experience he had with a high-level professor when he was an undergraduate that was particularly useful. He said the message to him was *"I see what you're doing. It's partially right and has potential. I believe you can do it; let me show you how."*

A second important research-based principle draws from Lev Vygotsky's (1978) seminal research on learning. Vygotsky, a developmental psychologist, posited that learning occurs through two systems: cognition and social interaction. He theorized that we build learning from a student's current level of understanding and interaction. This concept is known as the *zone of proximal development*. There are two points to consider when applying this principle. First, students come to school at different stages of cognitive development. For example, Ernest is teaching ninth-grade students who are about the same chronological age; however, their level of cognitive development in terms of the biological concepts being taught varies widely. Some have a solid understanding about cells and reproduction, while others are just beginning to grasp these concepts and the vocabulary associated with them. Simultaneously, and to our second point, some students may have had a good deal of communicative experience engaging in the type of interactions that are used/required in courses of study (e.g., how a science experiment is written in Ernest's class), whereas others have not. Students must be supportively mentored/apprenticed to advance their thinking and communication skills.

While these research-based principles have generally been applied to what we as educators do with our students, it is critical to consider our greatest partners in a child's education, their families, as well as the resources available in our classroom and school communities and our communities at large.

REFLECTION ACTIVITIES

Time for Reflection

Reflect on the following question and write a response.

Discuss two activities that you might do that reflect the relationship-focused perspectives presented in this chapter.

1.

2.

Valuing the Assets Within and Beyond the Classroom

For some of our students, the literacy and interactive activities that are practiced in their homes closely match our own as well as the culture of the schools in which we work (Epstein et al., 2009; Faltis, 2001;

Henderson, Mapp, Johnson, & Davies, 2007; Zacarian, 2013). The match continuously supports this group of students to engage in the type of interactions that are of social value and result in empowerment in school. Shirley Bryce Heath (1983) and Lisa Delpit's (1995) seminal research in home and school language reveals the differences between certain groups. Their research findings have helped our field see that we often associate groups that are distinct from the dominant culture, such as poor families and families who do not practice literacy culture, as having less value and power. Unfortunately, this false perception pays little attention to the rich assets that this group brings to their children's learning; the benefits of building partnerships with families from diverse cultural, language, and economic experiences; and the importance of extending learning beyond school. The research shows that family, peers, and members of the school community and the community at large are outstanding resources for student learning and empowerment when we involve them in this process (Epstein et al., 2009).

Let's return to Ernest's biology class and the suggestions that we have given him. Before he read them, he did not believe that some of his students could do the homework assignments he assigns because he knows that some of their parents, in his words, "are not literate"— meaning that he worries that some parents are not able to read, understand what he is assigning, and help their children to complete these homework assignments. Drawing from the research, we suggest that for homework his students explain their small group's project to a family member or friend, note the questions and/or ideas that they are asked about it, and bring these to the subsequent class. We further suggest that for Curriculum Night Ernest engage families in activities. One that perhaps you might have suggested in the reflection space is for parents/guardians to gather in small groups to collaboratively write a note to the students about what they learned from their projects. Doing this well may require our thinking of diverse approaches to this task, especially with parents/guardians who might not be literate in English. While translators can be helpful, videos and other media can also support this activity. During Curriculum Night, for example, groups of parents videotaped messages to Ernest's students. Whatever creative means there are to gather parents/guardians is helpful. We suggest this because the research that we have presented thus far shows the critical importance of interaction.

Moll, Amanti, Neff, and Gonzalez (1992) provide us with some important findings. They studied family and school communities living in the border region between the United States and Mexico and found that all family members possessed high levels of knowledge and skills that related to their work, home, and well-being and, more important, that they passed these on to their children. Moll et al. coined the term *funds of knowledge* to describe families' expertise in a wide variety of areas such as agriculture, business, repair, and medicine. They also point to the possibilities that can occur when educators intentionally draw from the funds of knowledge of their students' home communities. We believe that these networks of possibilities can be made even stronger when we call on the resources in our classroom communities, including students, families, and ourselves; our school community, including older students, fellow teachers and staff, parents, and other school-based resources; and the community at large.

Each of these potentially provides us with many possibilities for rich interactions for students to develop stronger cognitive and linguistic skills. Also, their involvement and support has measurable impact on student success (Epstein et al., 2009; Moll et al., 1992). An example of this is encouraging families to support their children in subject matters that they do not know about, such as calculus. How can this occur? While families might not possess knowledge in the subject, they do know how to support their child's particular efforts and perseverance to obtain this specialized knowledge and skill.

REFLECTION ACTIVITIES

Time for Reflection

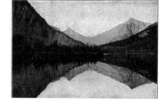

Reflect on the following question and write a response.

Provide two or three examples of how you might draw from the various assets of a classroom, school, or community at large to interactively practice with the family community the biology concepts that Ernest is teaching.

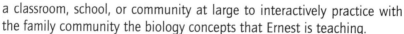

1.

2.

3.

Summary

In this chapter, we presented research-based principles about the importance of making connections, keeping students' stress levels low, and valuing the assets and resources within and beyond our classrooms. Key to realizing the effects of these principles are the ways in which we are mindful about the processes that must be put into play to make this work for our diverse learners. In our next chapter, we will introduce some of the key concepts for laying the foundation for an active and participatory classroom community.

References

Cannon, W. B. (1927). *Bodily changes in pain, hunger, fear and rage: An account of recent researches into the function of emotional excitement.* New York, NY: D. Appleton.

Delpit, L. (1995). *Other people's children: Cultural conflict in the classroom.* New York, NY: New Press.

Epstein, J., Sanders, M. G., Sheldon, S. B., Simon, B. S., Salinas, K. C., Rodrigues Jansorn, N., . . . Williams, K. (2009). *School, family, and community partnerships: Your handbook for action* (3rd ed.). Thousand Oaks, CA: Corwin.

Faltis, C. (2001). *Joinfostering: Teaching and learning in multicultural classrooms.* Upper Saddle River, NJ: Merrill Prentice Hall.

Foote, C. J., Vermette, P. J., Wilson-Bridgman, J., Sheeran, T. J., Erwin, R., Murray, M. (2004). Preparing secondary teachers to use cooperative learning strategies. In E. G. Cohen, C. Brody, & M. Sapon-Shevin, (Eds.), *Teaching cooperative learning: The challenge for teacher education* (pp. 97–110). Albany: State University of New York Press.

Freire, P. (1970). *Pedagogy of the oppressed.* New York, NY: Herder and Herder.

Heath, S. B. (1983). *Ways with words: Language, life, and work in communities and classrooms.* New York, NY: Cambridge University Press.

Henderson, A. T., Mapp, K. L., Johnson, V. R., & Davies, D. (2007). *Beyond the bake sale: The essential guide to family-school partnerships.* New York, NY: New Press.

Jensen, E. (2008). A fresh look at brain-based education. *Phi Delta Kappan, 89,* 408–417. doi:10.2307/20442521

Moll, L. C., Amanti, C., Neff, D., & Gonzalez, N. (1992). Funds of knowledge for teaching: Using a qualitative approach to connect homes and classrooms. *Theory Into Practice, 31*(2), 132–141. doi:10.1080/00405849209543534

Nation, I. S. P. (2001). *Learning vocabulary in another language.* Cambridge, UK: Cambridge University Press.

Steele, C. M. (2010). *Whistling Vivaldi and other clues to how stereotypes affect us.* New York, NY: W. W. Norton.

Sylwester, R. (2010). *A child's brain: The need to nurture.* Thousand Oaks, CA: Corwin.

Vasquez, V. (2014). *Negotiating critical literacies with young children* (10th anniv. ed.). New York, NY: Routledge.

Vygotsky, L. (1978). *Mind in society* (M. Cole, Trans.). Cambridge, MA: Harvard University Press.

Zacarian, D. (2011). *Transforming schools for English learners: A comprehensive framework for school leaders.* Thousand Oaks, CA: Corwin.

Zacarian, D. (2013). *Mastering academic language: A framework for supporting student achievement.* Thousand Oaks, CA: Corwin.

4

Preparing for
Classroom Community

*Instruction begins when you, the teacher, learn from the learner;
put yourself in his place so that you may understand . . . what he
learns and the way he understands it.*

— Soren Kierkegaard (Thompte, 2009, p. 201)

> What are the first steps in getting to know a new class of students and
> their families in advance of their arrival in school? Why are these useful
> and important to do, and how can a teacher begin to do this? To consider
> these questions, let's look at how third-grade teacher Gabriela Cintrón
> begins this process.

Gabriela Cintrón is a third-grade classroom teacher in a suburban
community south of Phoenix, Arizona. She is coming to school
for the first time since the previous school year. She is just beginning
to put her toe in the water by going into the office to get her new class
list. She reads through the roster to get a first level of information that
helps her begin thinking about the physical space for the learning
needs of this new group.

Asking Questions About the Classroom Community

In addition to gathering the class roster, Gabriela has found some activities to be particularly helpful for starting the school year. One of the most important ones is to assemble a list of questions that she has about her new community of students. Figure 4.1 shows the questions that Gabriela forms as she reads her new class roster:

Figure 4.1 Gabriela's List of Questions About Her New Students

- How many students are on the roster?
- How many have individualized educational plans (IEPs) that require physical accommodations in the classroom?
- What is the nature of the accommodations?
- Who may need an amplification system, visual supports, preferential seating, and/or distinct separated workspaces?
- How many students are English learners?
- How many support staff may need desks or work spaces in the classroom?
- Are there students with therapeutic needs who require rest or exercise areas apart from general areas?

The answers to these questions and others will help Gabriela set up the physical space of her classroom, including the number of desks and chairs, modifications, tools and planning arrangements, as well as how these factors will form the basic floor plans of her classroom.

REFLECTION ACTIVITIES

Time for Reflection

Reflect on the following question and write a response.

Consider the questions that Gabriela poses in Figure 4.1 as she reads her new class roster.

1. Which questions do you think are most important from your perspective? Why?

2. What questions help you see things in an unexpected way?

3. List three additional questions that you might want answers to and the reasons why you think that these are important to ask.

   a.

   b.

(Continued)

> (Continued)
>
>   c.

Aside from the competing demands for time to get her room physically ready for the school year, Gabriela knows that it is essential for her to develop, nurture, and facilitate partnerships. It is one of her primary goals in starting the school year. The preparation that she undertakes in getting to learn about a group of students is similar to the kind of research that an actor or novelist might do to prepare for creative work and a historian might do to better understand a period in time. She begins by researching available written records, student photos, report cards, written artifacts of student work, conference notes, test scores, and family demographics and jots her findings in a notebook of observations about her new community. She makes predictions about the students that she is about to inherit, particularly those who because of academic performance or social/emotional challenges appear to need a higher degree of a teacher's attention and understanding. Like a historian, she also does fact-finding interviews with colleagues and students' families with whom she can connect to address the most urgent questions, curiosities, and potential complications that she has formed about her future class community. These connections include the students' previous year's teachers, guidance counselors, building administrators, and, most vitally, her students' parents/guardians.

This information gathering helps Gabriela form a picture of her developing classroom community by being proactive in an informed and responsive way. It takes extra work and time to do this type of planning. However, she has found it is well worth the effort. Gabriela reflects that she has done this work before and at the beginning of the school year depending on the time that she has available and what her school's policies allow. Her efforts, she believes, make her work much more productive and make her feel much more up to the challenge of starting the school year. She then assembles a list of questions in different categories to help her understand her incoming students' needs, challenges, and strengths. The following section discusses the types of information and questions that Gabriela knows are important to consider.

Asking Questions About Diverse Learners and Learning Needs

Among the students in Gabriela's classroom community, who are the students with identified special education needs? What does each one's IEP call for Gabriela to know? Who are the English learners in her class? What are their language backgrounds? What do the home language surveys and/or other documents state about the language(s) in which parents/guardians can communicate with her? If she is not sure about this information, she makes a note of this to be sure that she can secure it (as she wants to ensure that face-to-face and written communication occurs in languages that families can communicate in). What are the English language development levels of the English learners? Has their education been interrupted? Where did they attend school previously? How many students in her class will be receiving free or reduced lunch? What types of considerations should Gabriela make for the students in her class that live in poverty? Are there students who live in shelters? Who are the teachers and staff that will also work with Gabriela's students (such as special education staff, teachers of English learners, occupational and physical therapists, and counselors)? Will they be working in or taking students out of her classroom? What are the space and furniture needs of teachers, aides, and others who might be joining her classroom community?

Physical Space Needs

While Gabriela knows that she has to carefully consider the physical needs of some of her students and that a good deal of her back-to-school activities involve preparing her room, she also knows that information gathering is essential. This includes learning about any student with medical needs requiring a particular type of attention or awareness from her and students with hearing, sight, or physical mobility/wheelchair needs requiring her to provide preferential seating, wider aisles for unrestricted access to the room, and other accommodations. It also requires that she know about students with sensory needs or a high need for frequent movement.

Emotional Issues

Is there a history of conflicts among particular students? Are there predictable ways that certain students have responded to academic demands? Have they engaged in patterns of behavior that required frequent intervention from a guidance or therapeutic counselor? What initiatives helped these students the most? What social-emotional skills have they begun to develop? What existing relationships with adults remain important to students and can be called on to offer additional support and guidance that they may need?

Challenges Due to Family Circumstances

Have challenges to the adults in a student's family impacted the stability of his/her life? This might include: divorces or remarriages, changes in child custody, loss of income/job, natural disaster, and/or emotional crisis that has required a student to cope in ways that are not typical to a child's development. Are there events in a student's recent family history that may affect performance in school? Does a student have food or clothing needs that have required help from social services or the school community? This is the sort of information that does not appear in records, but has profound implications for the kinds of teacher supports that are necessary to offer to particular students so that they may be better supported and more successful in their learning.

Reviewing Information to Make Informed and Thoughtful Decisions

The initial information that Gabriela gathers is powerful. It allows her to take appropriate measures proactively (before problems emerge) rather than in response to a problem. If they are fortunate, teachers may have some time before students arrive to speak to the previous year's teachers or other school staff and to begin forming a picture. Because of the sensitive nature of most of these topics, it is generally not appropriate to share these observations in emails or written form to help safeguard the privacy and confidentiality of families and their children.

Gabriela studies the pictures of her incoming students (if these are available). She learns the pronunciation of the names that they use with classmates and teachers (not just the official formal names on records) so that when folders, cubbies, and signs in the classroom are labeled, they use the children's "real" names. Such attention to detail allows her to greet students with familiarity from their first meeting. It is an opportunity for her to begin to know and care about these students. It is also a way for her to build a foundation of trust from the very first interactions that she has with students and families, so they'll know that she cares and sees them and their specific needs and strengths. Gabriela describes it this way:

A CLOSER LOOK
Gabriela Cintrón

I feel like the preparation that I do in pre-learning about the students is as important as any preparation for lessons that I might ever do. It is the basis for building relationships with them and their families, because I start to see them as individuals and can communicate to students and their guardians that they are known and seen. It's an investment of time that I make that helps me create the kind of start that I most want for the year—one in which my appreciation and affection for students is developing even before the first day, I'm establishing trust with them and their families as I make a first impression, and I can avoid as many big surprises as possible. Starting a new school year is like starting a new business. And just like businesses need to have capital on hand and credit, a teacher needs the credit of trust and the capital of relationship and detailed information about the students and families we serve.

She notes that it can be a challenge to attend to the time-consuming details of gathering materials and organizing desks and displays and planning lessons *and* manage to learn about students and families in a detailed way. However, she has come to realize that the time she invests in learning about the students and families and reaching out to them before and/or as the year starts makes the year richer and more successful.

REFLECTION ACTIVITIES

Time for Reflection

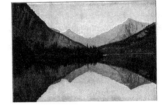

Reflect on the following question and write a response.

Who are two or three staff members in your school/district that you could talk to about students in an incoming class?

1.

(Continued)

(Continued)

2.

3.

List three questions that you would be sure to ask these resources about students. Consider areas such as academic needs, physical needs, social-emotional needs, and the needs brought about by family circumstances.

1.

2.

3.

Setting a Reassuring, Positive, and Safe Tone

Gabriela invests time to communicate with families while she is physically setting up the classroom. She has noted the families that require communication in a language other than English and is working diligently with school resources to provide written and oral translation support. The interactions, as we will see, include mail/email, phone calls, and meetings with her future students and their families. Translating them into the families' various home languages and having a trusted translator who represents the language and culture of families is a critical component to this work.

These communications serve many important functions. They demonstrate to families her willingness to meet with them and their child out of curiosity, respect, and conscientiousness. They are also intended as an invitation to see a school-home partnership as an alliance created out of common interest to support a shared concern: the students' well-being. This sets a reassuring and safe tone for the school year, even before it begins, and can positively affect all that happens afterward.

Gabriela has found that these depend on essential factors including the amount of time that teachers are afforded by their school district and the ways in which teachers choose to do these contacts on their own time. Like many educators, Gabriela finds that the type of activities that she does before or as the school year begins range in low to high investments of time. Figure 4.2 provides a sampling of the types of activities that can be accomplished before or in the beginning of the school year. We have separated these into two columns: low and high time investment.

Figure 4.2 Methods of Pre-year Contact

Low Time Investment	High Time Investment
Simple postcard mailing or email contact	Phone calls
Welcome letter	Home visits
	Questionnaire
Welcome note on teacher's/school's/ staff's website	30-minute Open House activity

Low-Investment Activities

This section provides samples of activities that require low time investment. Each is intended for reaching out to families and students for introductions and welcome. The first activity is a postcard. This is the easiest form of contact. It is simply a message of greeting from the teacher to the student and family to open the channel of communication and establish a positive tone. Figure 4.3 shows a postcard that Gabriela sent to her students and their families.

Figure 4.3   Postcard Greeting

Dear Parents and Student,

Welcome to my class! I am looking forward to working with you this year and am excited for the school year to begin. I can be reached at this email during the school year: mCintron@yourchildsschool.edu. I look forward to meeting you soon.

Sincerely,

Mrs. Cintrón

Figure 4.4 is a letter that Gabriela sent/emailed to her new students and their families. The purpose of a letter is not too different from that of the postcard. It is a means to welcome families and students to a new classroom.

Figure 4.4   Informational Letter to Elementary School Students and Parents

---

Dear Parents and Students,

I am excited for the year ahead! Along with this message of welcome, I am writing to send the first of my regular classroom letters to you.

I want to extend an invitation to all Room 24 parents and families to take part in our classroom activities throughout the year. Here are some of the ways that parents and families can join.

- Helping us go on field trips
- Assisting with art, cooking, or special projects
- Mentoring and tutoring children in class
- Making special presentations that tie in with our studies
- Showing us your craft, work, or workplace
- Helping assemble and type books created by students
- Helping display student work
- Donating materials such as containers, snacks, or surplus books and magazines
- Coming to special events and performances

You might have additional ideas and I encourage you to share these with me. I greatly value families participating in our classroom community and am looking forward to a happy and rewarding year of learning together!

Warmly,

Gabriela Cintrón

A similar letter for the parents and families of middle and high school students would look somewhat different to reflect the needs of older students. Figure 4.5 shows a sample from a high school mathematics teacher.

Figure 4.5   Informational Letter to Middle or High School Students and
Parents

Dear Parents and Students,

I am excited for the year ahead! Along with this message of welcome, I am
writing to send the first of my regular classroom letters to you.

I want to extend an invitation to parents and families to participate throughout
the year. Here are some of the ways that you can join us.

- Come to special events, programs, or performances.
- Encourage, mentor, and support students to complete homework or
  classroom assignments.
- One of my most important goals is that your child is successful in my
  class. Please encourage him or her to let me know when they need
  instructional support.
- Volunteer to be involved in classroom or schoolwide service projects.

You might have additional ideas, and I encourage you to share these with me.
I greatly value families participating in our classroom community and am looking
forward to a happy and rewarding year of learning together!

Warmly,

[Teacher's name]
Mathematics teacher

Many schools include a webpage or section for individual teachers. Keith Maletta, English teacher at Central Cabarrus High School in
Concord, NC, includes the welcome message in Figure 4.6 in his
effort to help build relationships with his incoming students.

Figure 4.6   Welcome Note on High School Teacher's Webpage

I was born on Long Island, N.Y., where I lived for twelve years until my parents
decided the country was the place they wanted to be, so they loaded up the Ford
and we moved north to the metropolis of Lake Luzerne. After high school, I
attended S.U.N.Y @ Oswego. Go, Great Lakers!

I taught for a year at St. Mary's Academy in Rensselaer, NY and then
escaped the weather and moved south in 1993. Fortunately, I was hired here at
Central Cabarrus High School. After twenty years, I consider this more than a
school; it's a second home.

When I'm not teaching English and cracking corny jokes, I spend time with
my family, drive my awesome "S.U.V." (aka "Sport Utility Van") to my sons'
numerous activities, search out new music online, play way too much fantasy
football, and attempt to get my 44-year-old self into shape.

In addition to teaching, I work with Ms. Meehan, Ms. Norris, and Ms.
Schmidt, helping to facilitate Central's Link Crew, a group of 90
upperclassmen leaders who act as mentors for incoming freshmen.

I look forward to meeting all of you and beginning another great year here at
Central Cabarrus High School, but you better get used to me talking about my
favorite teams: the New York Yankees, the Carolina Panthers, the Carolina Hurricanes,
the Michigan Wolverines, and my graduate alma mater, the Charlotte 49rs!

Source: Cabarrus County Schools (2014).

High-Investment Activities

In addition to or in lieu of low-investment activities, the following high-investment activities take time and are solidly worth it! They greatly help to set a welcoming and open tone. They also help to give a purpose and intentionality to the work of teaching and building community around the classroom.

Phone Contact

Phone calls can be an important mechanism for welcoming new families and students. They serve the same purpose as sending a postcard or a letter and can be preceded by these activities to let parents know that a phone call will be made and when it will happen. Phone calls allow for interaction and conversation. While not all families have phones and the phone numbers that schools have may not be working numbers all of the time, it is a potentially powerful activity to consider. Also, it is essential to know that some students are in the care of more than one custodial parent or family community members (e.g., grandparents during the day, parent at night), some might not have a phone or be reachable at all, and some may require that a translator make the call on your behalf. Despite all of these productive tensions, one strategy for making this an important and manageable plan is to ensure that the sole purpose is to focus on the priority of welcoming new students and their families and to try to limit calls to 5 minutes or less.

As with the postcard and letter, it is helpful to have a flexible script ready for the first call. Gabriela's phone call script appears in Figure 4.7. She is not sure whether she will reach voice mail, a parent/guardian, or the child. She is ready for any outcome by using her flexible script.

Figure 4.7   Phone Call Script

Hello, this is Gabriela Cintrón and I am [student name's] new teacher. I wanted to call to welcome you to my classroom.

- I also wanted to invite you to come to [upcoming event, such as potluck supper].

- I hope we get to meet in person soon. I am excited for the year ahead!

- In the meantime, please feel free to contact me at [school phone/email/contact information] with any questions, information, concerns, or messages that you would like me to know.

Beginning-of-the-Year Survey or Questionnaire

In addition to the postcard and letter, Gabriela also sends families a survey with questions that allow parents of elementary school students to share personal insights and what they feel is important about their child's life. By asking these questions, Gabriela communicates that this information matters to her. She intentionally opens a channel for communication that is caring and personal. Secondary students and their families can also participate directly in a teacher's or school's request for information. These activities are not intended to be intrusive; they are to help teachers get to know students and their families as whole people in ways that school records do not always show and school staff might not know. For younger students, the information that parents share may include learning style, likes and dislikes, friendship issues, and events in the child's life that families want their child's new teacher to know. For older students, the information obtained about them and their families may be just as important. Figure 4.8 provides a sample of the type of survey or questionnaire that Gabriela uses. She creates it for her self-contained grade-level elementary school classroom, but it can be adapted for team use and, of course, use at the secondary level. The information is intended as a tool to gain personal insights about her students and for families to feel welcomed into a caring partnership with her.

Figure 4.8 Beginning-of-the-Year Survey for Parents

Child's name: _____

Parent/guardian name(s): _____

Addresses and phone numbers of where school information should be sent:

Primary address and phone: _____

Additional address and phone (if applicable):

_____

Email: _____

   Your insights about your child are really important and useful to me as I get to know her/him. We will have other chances (such as conferences) to talk, but I invite you to jot down whatever you'd like me to know as the new year starts. Use an additional sheet of paper if you need to.

(Continued)

Figure 4.8   (Continued)

1. What would you like me to know and understand about your child?

2. What is she/he enthusiastic about at home? What games and activities is she/he drawn to? What characters or stories from books, movies, or TV does she/he like?

3. Are there specific things you would like to see her/him get special support with this year?

Secondary teachers can also engage in beginning-of-the-year activities that are targeted for the same purpose: gaining information about students to support our work with them. Keith Malletta, for example, furnishes every student with an index card to respond to a list of questions that he asks during the first week of school. He then uses these student-created cards as a means of getting to know and work with his students. Figure 4.9 provides the list of questions that Keith Malletta asks.

Figure 4.9   Keith Malletta's Questions

- Activities you're involved with at Central Cabarrus High School
- Activities you do at home
- Rate yourself as an editor (1–5). FIVE is strongest [E = 5]
- Rate yourself as a writer (1–5). [W = 4]
- Rate yourself as a reader (1–5). [R = 5]
- Rate yourself as a communicator (1–5). [R = 5]
- Rate your ability to get along with others (1–5). [G = 5]

Elena Aguilar (2012) provides the following list of survey questions that she has found helpful in starting the school year. You may wish to select some of these using an index card format such as Keith uses, include all of these, or add some of your own.

- Tell me about a teacher you really liked and what he or she did that you appreciated.
- Tell me about a teacher that you felt wasn't effective and why.
- What do you think makes a "good" teacher?
- Describe the most interesting activity you ever did in school.
- Describe the most challenging class or unit of study.
- How do you like to get feedback?
- If I notice that you're not following one of our classroom agreements, how would you like me to let you know?
- On a scale of 1–5, how much do you like reading? (1 = *not at all*, 2 = *sort of/sometimes*, 3 = *most of the time*, 4 = *I like reading*, 5 = *I LOVE reading*)
- On a scale of 1–5, how would you rate your reading skills? (1 = *I'm a terrible reader*, 2 = *I'm not a very good reader*, 3 = *I'm an OK reader*, 4 = *I'm a good reader*, 5 = *I'm a really, really good reader*)
- What did you read last year in school or outside of school?
- Who do you know who likes to read?
- Outside of school, who do you think believes in you and supports you most?
- Who do you want me to tell when you do really well in school?
- Tell me about something that's been hard for you in your life.
- Tell me about something you feel proud of.
- Tell me about something you love doing that has nothing to do with school.
- What's your favorite thing to do on the weekend?
- If you could have three wishes, what would they be?
- What would you like to know about me?
- What else can you tell me that would help me be a better teacher to you? (Aguilar, 2012)

Optional-But-Useful Relationship-Building Activities

Open House Early in the School Year

It can be greatly helpful for parents and students to meet teachers and visit classrooms early in the year, or ideally before the first day of school, if your situation permits. It can also be helpful to use this time for students and parents to meet each other. An Open House for this purpose helps to set the stage for community building. It can easily be arranged through a mailed or emailed invitation and/or a phone call (depending on what we know about the type of parent communication that works best). Figure 4.10 provides a sample of a letter that Gabriela sends/emails to parents inviting them and their child to an Open House event in her classroom. Some teachers, if time permits and the school allows, may find this useful to do before the school year, while preparing their rooms for the first day of school, and others may find it helpful to do at the beginning of the year. The idea is that families and students can visit and take part in an activity that contributes to the preparation, such as putting labels on folders, drawing or writing something that can be put in a "getting to know you" display, and more. As seen in the sample in Figure 4.10, the Open House invitation, sent several weeks before the start of the school year, includes a date, start time, and end time. While it is targeted to elementary school teachers, it can be adapted for middle and high school students. In addition, home visits may be prioritized for students who are most at risk.

Figure 4.10   Open House Invitation

Dear Families,

I am greatly looking forward to working with you, your child, and our class community. I am writing to invite you and your child to visit our classroom on Monday, [date and time, such as 1:00–1:45], the day before school starts.
   I am happy to be your child's teacher and look forward to our year together!

Sincerely,

Gabriela Cintrón

Home Visits

The practice of home visits by teachers is not always practical in all circumstances. The family's home situation may make visiting difficult or, in some cases, not desirable or feasible. It is also a practice that goes beyond the usual boundaries of the teacher's professional role. However, it has the potential to be transformative in unconventional ways and can greatly help us achieve what we are in teaching to do: help our students, be successful in school, their community, and beyond.

In Chapter 1, we introduced Pink's (2009) ideas and the benefits that we gain from figuring out, for ourselves, what works for our students. Home visits have the power to help us gain invaluable insights about our students and families and build powerful relationships with them. What do we mean? Let's look at Thomas Holtzberg, a high school mathematics teacher whose ninth-grade algebra class has many students who seem unmotivated to learn the content. While he has taken many professional development courses on making math more meaningful, Thomas has found it very challenging to find ways to ensure that his students will learn the math content. This has affected his motivation. A colleague suggested that he visit the homes of some of these students as a means of helping them and their families know how much he cares. After conducting a few visits, Thomas found that his students were far more invested in learning. While he does not have to do these activities, they have been an innovative way to support him in his work and increase his investment in teaching.

A home visit can be a means to establish trust and demonstrate to the student (and the family) that the teacher is a person in the student's life who understands the student as a whole person, who cares about her or him not just as a producer of test results, or as a worker, but almost as a family member would—as a caring adult taking responsibility not required by the job but inspired by personal caring and emotional involvement.

Home visits allow the teacher to get information and understanding that might not be available any other way. This information comes in many forms from what is said, to what is on the walls, to where people sit, to the family's attitude about the visit, to how parents redirect students about how to behave during the visit (or do not need to at all). All of this information provides a wealth of background knowledge. It proves useful in creating classroom plans and unraveling future mysteries about students' learning, behavior, and/or emotional challenges during the course of the school year. It also helps in understanding a range of additional information such as family dynamics, books that are available to the child, the responsibilities the child has, the flavor of family relationships, the cultural artifacts that suggest what is important to the family, and what influences are prominent in the child's life.

To conduct home visits well, we believe that there must be a plan to set the tone of caring (e.g., "I'll come for about 20 minutes. I'll sit down with your child and the rest of the family, if you prefer, and do a mini-interview with them, providing time for you to meet me and ask questions."). We also believe that it can be helpful to provide families, in advance, with some questions that might be discussed so that they can feel prepared and ready and not awkward. The responses to these questions help to provide insights about how parents view their child and about important but personal information such as medical conditions or situational changes that may have a behind-the-scenes impact on a child's day-to-day emotions or functioning as a student. In addition to preparing for the meeting, it can also be helpful to keep a journal about home visits. This can be a helpful means for noting what went well and what needs strengthening.

One of us, Michael, regularly keeps a journal of home visits. Let's have a look at a sample of Michael's journal entry to better understand the ways in which he prepared for pre-year home visits and his self-reflection after they occurred.

A CLOSER LOOK
Michael's Journal

8/20/13 Goals for today

I'll be visiting with students in their homes and doing some key visits with children who are going to need a lot of support to succeed this year. I realize that even though I am meeting with the student, the visit is also to send a message to the family that I can be trusted to care beyond the customary definition of a teacher's role to teach in school during school hours. It almost doesn't matter what else I say after "hello," as long as I feel tuned in to curiosity and making a cordial and warm connection.

I know that once the year starts and I have to start identifying areas of challenge, and ways the student and family need to put in extra effort, it is going to be helpful to have the request from someone who has shown they are willing to go the extra mile.

If nothing else, I want to convey that the well-being and success of their child matters to me in my heart and that we have this in common. Everything else I do in these meetings, like gather useful information and insights that will help in the future, is a plus.

Some questions I can ask the student:

- What do you want to learn or get better at or explore?
- What do you enjoy doing when you have a chance?
- What stories do you like to listen to when you are read to?
- What do you like to read?
- What have you done in school that gave you a good feeling?
- Do you have a favorite sport?
- Do you have a favorite game?
- Is there something you want me to know about you?
- Is there something you've done that you're proud of?
- Bring photos: Yearbook pictures of the class, of my family and dog. Ask them, "What do you want to know about me?"

8/23/13 How it actually went yesterday

Today, I saw four more students in person. I made appointments with four others to come to school for one-on-one visits. The rest, I hope, will come to the pre-year open house, though I know there are quite a few families that get in last trips and visits right up to the day school starts. I think things went uniformly pretty well. I felt myself communicating the warmth that I felt. It helped to go in with a plan. My plan was to find out favorite characters or books that they like to read or have read aloud by parents; favorite sport; favorite game; favorite interest. I also wanted to give them a chance to ask questions.

In following the plan, I felt like I let them know they mattered to me and that I am ready to go the extra mile. I also made sure to invite family involvement. I think (hope) I created a "buzz" about school starting, in a good way. I feel like I got at least half the kids and families feeling that we're on the same side before the kids even step in the door. That's huge.

I also learned about the home environments of the students: Kamal's plot in the family garden; Jordan's parents; Sally's musician parents and how Sally is interested in sitting next to the new girl, Sylvia, because she wanted to make new friends; David's parents actually went to my high school; Jon's kind mother and her boyfriend (his acting stepfather) helping deal with his disability; Larry's fragility and interest (obsession) with Legos; Maria's enthusiasm and friendliness; Jena standing on the couch and playing "Leaping Lizards" as I arrived and building things in the living room with wood and nails.

One thing I noticed about myself—I was sure. When I spoke to children, I gave them patient wait time for their answers. I was serious with them, but relaxed. I like my manner with them, actually, and I discovered it as I went, because I knew what I was about, and I trusted it. It gives me confidence to go into the year. I also liked how I said to parents: "We'll have time for blah-blah adult conversations later. I'll make sure you have my email and phone, but this is Sylvia's [or Theo's or Maria's] time. What feels good about this is that it was not calculated, but I can imagine that it is very strategic to communicate all this information and get all this information from children and families up front.

REFLECTION ACTIVITIES

Time for Reflection

1. What are the most essential messages and attitudes you would want to convey to families to set a tone for their involvement in the new school year?

(Continued)

(Continued)

2. What might you do to ensure that *all* families receive these messages given the different communications styles, home languages, and cultural expectations that you are likely to find among any group of school families?

3. Describe two action steps that you might take to get to know your students and their families' personal, social, cultural, home language, and world experiences so that you can draw from these in your work?

Laying the Foundation for a Community Around a Classroom

The activities described in this chapter represent a kind of immersion that starts before the students and teacher have fully begun their year together. Gabriela Cintrón, the teacher we presented at the beginning of this chapter, began her teaching career with a belief that the success of student learning, like all things human, is thoroughly influenced by the quality and consistency of social relationships that provide a context and purpose. She set about to create a situation in which students are surrounded by a teacher that knows them, parents that are involved in students' school and classroom life, parents know and sometimes even work together on behalf of the classroom, and the teacher knows the families.

This is a time when competing time pressures and demands on teachers, students, families, and schools seem to make voluntary investments in nonrequired activities more difficult. However, Gabriela acts from the conviction that the efforts she devotes to building relationships that support and recognize students' achievements and development will powerfully foster the well-being of those students. For this reason, she considers a core part of her work to be the facilitation of building relationships.

What she knows about learning and about motivation supports this. The involvement of families in classroom life increases the emotional importance of school for the child and for the parents. The effects of this amplify the motivations that students have to be members of the school and classroom community in its purpose to create a learning community to benefit them.

Summary

In this chapter, we presented the importance of pre-school-year activities. We provided ways to prepare for student-family community building through researching student files and meeting with prior teachers, counselors, and support staff. We also showed how to create pre-year activities that promote ways to build the foundation of a classroom community through various avenues of contact and communication.

In the next chapter, we will explore the cultural, linguistic, and personal assets of families as resources for the sociocultural, language/literacy, academic, and thinking development of students.

References

Aguilar, E. (2012). Listening to students. *Edutopia*. Retrieved from http://www.edutopia.org/blog/listening-to-students-elena-aguilar

Cabarrus County Schools. (2014). *Home: Faculty/staff: Maletta, Keith*. Retrieved from http://www.cabarrus.k12.nc.us/Domain/4471

Pink, D. (2009). *The surprising truth about what motivates us*. New York, NY: Penguin Books.

Thompte, R. (2009). *Kierkegaard's philosophy of religion*. Eugene, OR: Wipf and Stock.

5

The Academic Learning Benefits of Being "In It Together"

Every child deserves a champion—an adult who will never give up on them, who understands the power of connection, and insists that they become the best that they can possibly be.

—Rita Pierson (2013)

> How does the cultivation of trust, care, and empathy lead to successful engagement with the curriculum?

Mark Zimmerman is a 12-year veteran teacher who has depth of experience and training working with students from diverse racial, cultural, linguistic, and economic populations. We are watching him prepare a second-grade math lesson on odd and even numbers.[1] He has 23 students in his class with a range of mathematic abilities, half receive free or reduced lunch, 7 are English learners from diverse language backgrounds and countries of origin (including Latin and Central America and Vietnam), and 4 have identified special education needs,

---

[1]This scenario is drawn from Silverstone and Zacarian (2013).

including autism, a hearing impairment, auditory processing needs, and attention deficit disorders.[2] Some of his students come from homes where literacy is observed and practiced, while others come from homes where this is less common. Like many of us, Mark feels a good deal of pressure to ensure that he is adhering to, and that his students are keeping pace with, the performance standards that are expected of them. As a Massachusetts public school teacher, he is following the Common Core State Standards (CCSS) in Mathematics (Common Core State Standards Initiative, 2014) and the World-Class Instructional Design and Assessment (WIDA) amplification of the English language development standards (Board of Regents of the University of Wisconsin System, 2012). Here is what the CCSS second-grade mathematics standards require for the curriculum he is preparing to teach:

Represent and solve problems involving addition and subtraction.

CCSS.MATH.CONTENT.2.OA.A.1

Use addition and subtraction within 100 to solve one- and two-step word problems involving situations of adding to, taking from, putting together, taking apart, and comparing, with unknowns in all positions, e.g., by using drawings and equations with a symbol for the unknown number to represent the problem.

Add and subtract within 20.

CCSS.MATH.CONTENT.2.OA.B.2

Fluently add and subtract within 20 using mental strategies. By end of Grade 2, know from memory all sums of two one-digit numbers.

Work with equal groups of objects to gain foundations for multiplication.

CCSS.MATH.CONTENT.2.OA.C.3

Determine whether a group of objects (up to 20) has an odd or even number of members, e.g., by pairing objects or counting them by 2s; write an equation to express an even number as a sum of two equal addends.

Source: Common Core State Standards Initiative (2014).

---

[2]According to the Individuals with Disabilities Education Act, there are 13 disability types: autism, deaf-blindness, deafness, emotional disturbance, hearing impairment, intellectual disability, multiple disabilities, orthopedic impairment, other health impairment, specific learning disability, speech or language impairment, traumatic brain injury, and visual impairment (including blindness). Over the years, Mark has had students representing each of these categories.

Mark's district requires that he use the mathematics series *Investigations* (TERC, 2008) to teach this unit of study. Here is an excerpt from the course text.

Defining Even and Odd

Many young students become intrigued by the patterns they notice with evens and odds as they do work with whole numbers. An even number can be formally defined in several ways, including the following:

- A multiple of 2
- A number divisible by 2 (meaning a whole number that has no remainder when divided by two)
- A number that results from multiplying an integer by 2

In grade 2, student work in defining even and odd is grounded in partners and teams, a context that is closer to students' experience. In this context, an even number is defined as follows:

- A number that makes two equal teams or groups, with none left over
- A number that can be made into partners or pairs, with none left over

Second graders need to develop mental images as they think about and make sense of any definition. Therefore, it is important to model the above ideas with students using cubes and drawings.

Source: TERC (2008, p 151).

Mark's district also requires that he use the *2012 Amplification of The English Language Development Standards* (Board of Regents of the University of Wisconsin System, 2012) to instruct the English language learners in his class. To do this, he must carefully plan his math classes for the various English language development levels of his students. The levels include *Level 1—Entering, Level 2—Emerging, Level 3—Developing, Level 4—Expanding, Level 5—Bridging,* and *Level 6—Reaching* (p. 60). One of the 7 students is at Level 1, three are Level 4, and two are Level 5. According to the WIDA standards, students at Level 1 should "match words and phrases" (e.g., "more than," "less than," "take away . . . using illustrated word cards . . ."), students at Level 4 should "locate clues for solving problems . . . using realia with a partner," and students at Level 5 should "categorize word problems" (p. 60). As Mark plans his lessons, he carefully considers the types of tasks and activities that students at these various English language development levels can do.

In addition, he is required to follow the individualized education plans of each of the students in his class. Thus, before Mark plans his lessons, he must take the following factors into account in all that he does:

- His state's curriculum frameworks or standards (e.g., Common Core State Standards)
- Textbooks, materials, and other curricular resources that are guided by his district or school
- The regulations governing the education of English learners
- The individualized education plans of students with special education needs

Take a few moments to complete the following reflection activity.

REFLECTION ACTIVITIES

Time for Reflection

1. Reflect on the steps that Mark has taken thus far. What two additional steps or factors do you think are critical for him to take as he readies to teach?

2. What is the purpose(s) of the two additional steps or factors that you listed as critical for Mark to take?

In previous chapters, we explored the vital importance of creating a climate in which relationship and trust building are critical components as we undertake a school year. Now, we're going to take a look at specific ways the climate of trust and community that we have established can be utilized to promote the academic success of all learners. We also provide a range of examples from educators from across our country and label these "A Closer Look."

Our intent is to show how partnerships among students, teachers, and families as well as the classroom community, school community, and community at large can translate into productive interactions among students and bring the kinds of improved learning outcomes that education reform seeks but can never obtain through mandates alone. To begin our discussion, let's consider how this kind of cooperation can and does support learning. There are broad categories that we will cover in this discussion:

- imparting a positive message that all learners can learn
- understanding that all learners and families are smart and can contribute to learning
- making learning socially and personally relevant
- creating a caring community of learners
- understanding the process and task elements of academic interactions
- making learning visible and transparent
- using the support of the school community to make learning work
- working with the community at large to encourage learning

Imparting a Positive Message That All Learners Can Learn

In this book, we have referred to partnerships as the state of a relationship between two or more people. One of the most basic tenets of these relationships must be a culture of caring (Nodding, 2005). However, to be cared for in school settings implies two important conditions. The first is a belief that all learners can learn and that our classrooms are spaces in which we believe in them to do just that—be learners. In addition, it requires what Tosolt (2009) refers to as types of communication in which students and others (such as families) perceive that they are cared for. A challenge for many of us is that we may not be aware of the various cultural ways of communicating care other than our own.

The work of British psychologist John Bowlby (1969) outlines the early conditions that influence child development and care, what he referred to as *attachment theory*. During the first year of life, for example, a baby learns to draw on and develop expectations of reliable support from an adult caretaker. With repetition, consistency, and mutual responsiveness, the infant becomes attuned to the adult and secure, self-aware, and able to identify with the emotions of the caregiver. At the age of 5, when the child goes to school, the care that he or she has been receiving at home and elsewhere is expected to continue by the caring adults that the child will know as the teachers and others who will work with him or her in school. While certainly not all children come to school with the same experiences and a startling percentage have experienced or are experiencing trauma, violence, and chronic stress (Craig, 2008), we must consider the importance of student and family perceptions about how we care for them. This includes the ways in which we connect, respect, value, and honor our students' and families' personal, cultural, language, economic, and world experiences as well as differences in literacy, academic backgrounds, and understandings of how to think to learn (Zacarian, 2011, 2013).

An important step for understanding differences in perceptions is to acknowledge three types of underrepresented populations in the United States: autonomous, voluntary, and involuntary (Ogbu, 1992; Ogbu & Simons, 1998; Tosolt, 2009). The first includes ethnic groups, such as Irish and Italian, who are not racially different from dominant U.S. culture; the second includes those who came to the United States voluntarily, such as Japanese, Korean, and Chinese, who may experience discrimination but find the social structure of the dominant culture to be more favorable than the culture practiced in their home country; and the third group includes indigenous Americans as well as those who trace their ancestry to Africa, Mexico, and elsewhere and identify themselves as involuntary citizens (Tosolt, 2009). Research on student perceptions of teacher caring in terms of interpersonal, academic, and fairness found that the students who represented the dominant culture (the first two groups) perceived caring differently than did students from involuntary underrepresented experiences (Tosolt, 2009). This finding is quite relevant as we approach the concept of caring for our students and families, what this will look like, and how it will be demonstrated. A good means for doing this is to secure this information from our students and their families. Table 5.1 draws from the survey questions that Tosolt (2009) researched and offers examples of the types of information gathering that is essential.

Table 5.1   Students' Perceptions of Teacher Caring

Types of Caring From Teacher	Very Important	Important	Not very Important
Admits that he or she is wrong sometimes			
Helps me when other kids are picking on me			
Helps me with a problem not related to school			
Smiles at me			
Protects me			
Listens to my side of the story			
Gets involved when other students are being mean to each other			
Writes helpful comments on my writing			
Lets me ask lots of questions			
Holds classroom discussions that encourages a lot of student talk			
Holds me accountable for my school work			
Is known (by prior students and for years) to care about students			
Has ongoing relationships with students and families outside of school			
Offers support after school and/or during the summer months			
Is curious about me			
Enjoys teaching			
Makes effort to make school meaningful			
Makes effort to make classroom life enjoyable on a regular basis			
Cares about the subject(s) he or she teaches and wants me to have access to it in a generous way			

REFLECTION ACTIVITIES

Time for Reflection

Reflect on the following questions and write a response.

1. Complete the survey in Table 5.1 with a partner and discuss how your answers are the same or different.

2. Separate the survey questions into three categories—interpersonal, academic, and fairness—and discuss the importance of each in terms of creating a positive learning environment.

Let's look at the work of Kelley Brown to examine the importance of setting a positive tone.

A CLOSER LOOK
Kelley Brown

Kelley Brown is a Massachusetts history teacher of the year awardee who teaches at Easthampton High School in Easthampton, MA. About 30% of the district's students receive free or reduced lunch, 17% have been identified as having special education needs, and 4% have been identified as English learners. One of the areas that the district's high school is focusing on is engagement. We asked Kelley to describe how she encourages her students to be engaged. Rather than respond to the question, she posed it to her students. One 11th grader responded, "When the whole room is excited to learn, it makes everyone want to learn more."

Kelley reviewed the responses of all of her students and found some key areas that help them to be engaged in learning. One category that Kelley identified is setting the tone for positive interactions between herself and students and between students and their peers. She states that she does this intentionally so that her students know that their ideas, participation, and discussions are welcomed and wanted:

> When I asked students what made them want to be engaged in the classroom, the picture they created looked something like this: Engagement is fostered in a classroom that has a comfortable positive environment where no one is judged for his or her participation. The teacher is kind and knows how to connect with students on a personal and academic level.

In addition, Kelley states that there are certain dispositions that she tries to maintain on a daily basis.

> Every day I try to be kind, positive, and encouraging—always assuming the best about my students. Maintaining positivity is key to a classroom environment that is safe and worthy of engagement.
>
> Every day when my students enter I ask a simple question: "How is everybody doing?" And I give students a chance to respond. It gives me a quick assessment of the class to know if anyone is having a terrible day and allows us to settle in.
>
> Creating a positive classroom environment not only fosters engagement but is one answer to classroom management. My goal at the beginning of each semester is to establish "learning as the norm."

While it is important to impart a message that all learners can learn, the influence of creating a positive learning environment underscores the importance of helping students see that we value who they are as people and as learners. An essential means for conveying this message is taking the time to build strong relationships with our students (as well as their families, whenever possible). Kelley highlights the importance of these relationship-building efforts.

> Relationships are one of the fundamental ingredients for engagement. I like to get to know each student as a person and an individual learner. Most students in my class would say that I push them hard. I give them challenging and complex work and expect growth and effort, but I do so with compassion. If I expect my students to engage in difficult work, I need to be willing to spend time after school with them, return their emails, help them when they are frustrated, and really work to understand them as individual learners. I work every day to ensure that each student feels safe to participate and knows that I care about their learning and about them personally. When they do something well and show growth, I make sure to give them precise recognition and sometimes a sticker. High school students also really like stickers.

Understanding That All Learners and Families Are Smart and Can Contribute to Learning

Like Kelley Brown and Mark Zimmerman (the teacher described at the beginning of the chapter), most of us work in heterogeneous classroom settings where we are expected to differentiate instruction and attend to the various needs of our students "individually, equitably, and fairly" (Lotan, 2006, p. 33). Many of us, especially secondary teachers who teach well over 150 students a day, may see this as a daunting task! One way to approach it is to recognize, acknowledge, and value the rich assets of our student and family populations, what Rachel Lotan (2006) refers to as "smarts."

When we engage with others, we have perceptions about them and ourselves, and they do about us in relation to our status within the group. Cohen and Lotan (2014) describe these perceptions in terms of high and low status in relation to our self-perception and our beliefs about others academically, with peers, and/or in society. Two remedies have been found to be helpful for addressing issues of high and low status. First, we must acknowledge that there are many different types of intelligences and, second, a great place to find these is in all of our student and family communities. A key for bringing these intelligences to the work of learning is to closely observe, interview, and interact with our students and, whenever possible, their families. We should do this for various reasons.

It's very helpful to identify the strengths that each brings and to draw from these in the learning process. If we do this genuinely, it can help to support more than caring for our students and families— it can greatly support our caring for each other. Another important reason to observe, interview, and interact with students and families is to connect what is to be learned with what is meaningful for students.

Making Learning Socially and Personally Relevant

While it is important to follow the curriculum standards for all of our students, English language development standards for our English learners, and individualized educational plans of our students with disabilities, it is equally important to help all of them find meaning in learning. A helpful means for doing this is to secure ways to make learning socially and personally relevant for our students from a social justice perspective (Freire, 1993). While we might not consider this element in our planning and delivering lessons, it is an important opportunity to take.

Let's look back at Mark's plans for teaching a mathematics unit on odd and even numbers. How might he find a social justice issue in this mathematical concept? As he considers this, he observes that many of his students return from recess with a range of concerns, from the student who claims that a classmate is too bossy, to the student who appears to have no friends to play with, to the ever-present concern that there are behaviors on the playground that are "not fair." He begins to explore the concept of fairness and equity from the stance of what happens when his students feel like the "odd man out" versus when they feel included. He uses these ideas to help his students explore the mathematical concepts of odds and evens. He finds that approaching the concepts from this critical stance helps his students be more engaged in the topic being studied. He uses the language of math—*odd, even, making even teams,* and other terms, words, idioms and phrases—to support his students in using this language to describe what happens during recess when they feel included and part of the community. Thus, a key means for helping students feel invested in learning is to connect the content to be learned with issues that are meaningful and relevant to them. It is an invaluable stance that we, as thoughtful educators, have to develop. We must think and act with empathy about our students and their points of view and let this shape the learning experiences that we design for them.

REFLECTION ACTIVITIES

Time for Reflection

Reflect on the following questions and write a response.

1. Create a social justice element that relates the consequence of inequality to one or more of the following curricular themes to make learning more meaningful for students.

(Continued)

(Continued)

a. A middle school unit of study on the Civil War

b. A high school mathematics unit on probability

c. An elementary science lesson (of your grade-level choice) on the environment

Creating a Caring Community of Learners

Another important element is to expect that all members of a learning community will care for each other. Following this train of thought, an important feature of paired and groupwork is to expect differences of opinions, in learning habits and in interactions. Rather than using these as reasons to derail us from using this method, we must address issues as they occur so that we don't disturb the positive flow and purpose of interactive learning (Chiu, 2004). A caring, self-adjusting climate of cooperation is not just a matter of nipping in the bud things that go wrong, but of establishing a climate in which caring for the full range of community members, including the least able and most vulnerable, is demonstrated—paired with explicit protocols that show in advance how to handle tricky situations which might pose obstacles to trust or sharing of ideas.

Kelley Brown, our high school social studies teacher, discusses the tensions that she experiences in lowering the amount of time that she spends speaking and during which she is in control of her classes in favor of this method.

A CLOSER LOOK
Kelley Brown

For years I feared allowing students to have too much control in the classroom, because I did not trust their ability to guide us in the "right" direction. (I still fear it a little.) I have come to find, after years of practice, that the most engaging and successful student tasks require students to plan, make choices in their learning, make mistakes, and experience a healthy level of frustration. When asked about the most engaging activities in class, students overwhelmingly select the activities that include these ingredients. Simulations, mock conventions or hearings, and full-class Harkness discussions (developed by Philips Exeter Academy) top the students' lists of engaging activities. In a Harkness discussion, students have to answer an authentic historical question in a full-group discussion without teacher facilitation. They are asked to prepare different materials in relation to the question. All students have to participate relatively equally. They set the agenda, ask each other questions, analyze the material, share quotations, and formulate analysis related to the material and authentic question. All of this is done without the teacher. I sit on the side and take notes as they lead the way. In the end, they succeed or fail as a group, all receiving the same grade. None of these are easy tasks, usually requiring multiple steps, rewrites, and significant student risk, yet students find them engaging. And my formative and summative assessments show that students understand the material more deeply and over longer periods of time than with other tasks.

Creating a caring community of learners should not be confined to one classroom of learners. Rather, it's important to consider the whole community as potential participants in this process. Elise May, a theater/elocution specialist, and Susan Goldstein and Lucy Gable, English as a second language (ESL) teachers at Port Washington Union Free School District in New York, highlight some of the rich possibilities that can occur when cross-grade participants are included. They call their project "Multicultural Mentors: Building Community With English Language Learners (ELLs)." Here, they describe their goals for the program and some of the complexities that they encountered in achieving them.

A CLOSER LOOK
Elise May, Susan
Goldstein, and Lucy Gable

The Multicultural Mentors program was created to foster cultural exchange and mentorship for beginner-level ELLs at the elementary and secondary levels. Through grant funding provided by the Port Washington Education Foundation, ESL teachers and a theater/elocution specialist worked collaboratively to develop learning activities that would offer mutually enriching experiences to the elementary and secondary students. A goal of the mentorship is to enrich emotional growth and cultural awareness, which are significant components of the English as a second language curriculum at both the elementary and secondary levels. The program also supports students in improving their social language to achieve effective interpersonal communication. The theater/speech workshops create a safe, explorative environment that prepares all students for a culminating performance in English. The literacy experiences provide students with effective strategies for reading comprehension and developing their voices through written language.

While the teachers' goals helped them design the mentorship program, they encountered many productive challenges implementing it.

Building a sense of community across cultures, ages, and school buildings was a significant challenge. Video footage of our first session shows many students at the secondary level wouldn't speak, while one refused to attend. The elementary students were silent.

These challenges highlight that teaching is a dynamic process. While we can create what we believe are the best-laid plans (or textbooks can provide us with these), the actual enactment of them is highly dependent on our students' being *in it together* or engaged in the learning journey. When they are not, we must seek alternative solutions. This is where the craft of teaching comes into play and bears on our capacity to creatively build a community of engaged learners. Let's see what Susan Goldstein, Elise May, and Lucy Gable designed and did to make this possible and their thoughts about the outcomes.

Using a children's book titled *The Crayon Box That Talked* (Derolf & Letzig, 2011) as a mentor text to inspire and develop students' cultural voices reinforced the perspective that each student is unique. The text lent itself to the mentorship, allowing the secondary students to take on the role of narrator while the elementary students became different color crayons that initially didn't get along. During the project, students engaged in various modalities of reading and wrote personal narratives inspired by the mentor text, with the support of sentence prompts.

Peer-to-peer mentorship enriched writing lessons for the elementary participants, as high school students supported them in writing sentences about their unique qualities. In this writing exercise, we sought to honor the voices, backgrounds, and experiences of each student.

Video of the final performance demonstrates student growth on multiple levels and the development of a collaborative community. Allowing high school students to serve as cultural guides and mentors for younger students fostered agency in the high school students. Likewise, the elementary students served as a supportive, authentic audience for the high school students, developing their self-confidence. Upon reflection, an elementary student shared, "I learned to speak loudly and slowly," and a secondary student shared, "I learned that you never have to be shy when there are people in front of you."

Our sense of accomplishment was solidified when the student who initially was unwilling to participate in the program underwent an unexpected and remarkable transformation. Throughout the sessions, his participation became increasingly enthusiastic. When a high school student was ill on the day of the performance, the once-reluctant student confidently and calmly volunteered to perform the extra part. The supportive peer network that was cultivated in our learning community fostered a sense of ownership in this student, enabling him to stretch beyond his comfort zone and relish his success.

Understanding the Process and Task Elements of Academic Interactions

It is equally important to remedy status issues by intentionally separating students into diverse pairs or small groups (e.g., pairing boys with girls; pairing students from different language, cultural, ethnic, and economic experiences). This promotes our purpose of helping students understand the benefits of learning with and from each other and preparing them for a type of democratic citizenry that prepares them for life within and beyond school. To do this well requires that we take time to identify these issues and discuss some of the pitfalls or productive tensions that will occur beforehand as a normal part of any group's process in the work of learning together (Cohen & Lotan, 2014;

Zacarian, 1996, 2013). In looking at this closely, interactions with others involve a *process* element as well as a *product* or task element.

When we assign an interactive task, we should expect that students will come with beliefs and perceptions about their academic, peer, and societal status, work habits, and other behaviors as well as how the task should be completed. They will deliberate on the task based on these beliefs and perceptions unless we intervene and remedy problems as they occur. For the purpose of this discussion, let's say that the task that Mark Zimmerman assigns is for small groups to create three odd-even word problems. He should expect that differences or productive tensions can and will ensue when his student groups interact. James, a student in one of the groups, perceives himself and is perceived as having strong math skills and high status. When we observe him in the group that Mark has assigned, we hear James's voice more than anyone else's. Katya is also member of this group. She struggles in math and perceives that she has nothing to offer; we don't hear her interact in the group's process. What information might we explore with the class or with the group ahead of time so that their work together is as cooperative and respectful as possible?

The size of groups is important to consider. A practical suggestion is to limit them to no more than four or five so that students can first work in pairs or trios and then in small groups so that everyone has the opportunity to participate and is required to do so. An important means for encouraging equity in interaction is also the assignment of student roles (e.g., facilitator, note-taker). It also involves crafting careful instructions about the routines and practices that should occur when students engage in the groupwork. When students are involved in the formation of the routines and practices, their adherence to them may be heightened. We also have to think carefully about what we expect students to do in the process of interacting in an academic task. We want them to have conscious awareness. That is, we want our students to ask, "What will it look like when we are working well? What will it sound like when we are working well? What characteristics will define a quality outcome or product?"

Throughout our book, we have highlighted the importance of talking more or communicating more to learn more. Humans use language to perform a wide variety of functions, from expressing information and knowledge; to asking questions about the world around us; to expressing our feelings, opinions, and identity; to communicating our creative or imaginative ideas and more (Halliday, 1985; Peregoy & Boyle, 2008). Groupwork is an important method for providing these interactive opportunities. According to Elizabeth Cohen (2006), a scholar on heterogeneity and groupwork, there must be certain conditions for using this method. It should be used to engage in *conceptual thinking* tasks for understanding and applying ideas. It must also include the resources that students need to engage in this type of work. These include the thinking skills and language or vocabulary that we want students to use as well as any information that we know is needed for students to complete a task successfully. Knowing that this is necessary, Mark provides his students with clear learning tasks, content vocabulary, and models for expressing the thoughts behind the mathematical concepts. He also draws from the curricular standards, English language development standards, and his district's mathematics text to determine the learning goals and objectives, and he creates tasks and activities that will accomplish these.

Making Learning Visible and Transparent

Once we understand and value the importance of creating interactive learning spaces, it becomes essential to create tasks and activities that are transparent so that everyone (the student and others such as parents and the special education, bilingual, or ESL staff who work with the student) knows the learning goal. Learning tasks and activities must also be meaningful so that students can be invested and see value in learning. To be effective, they should also allow students to have control over their learning. Kelley Brown, our high school social studies teacher, discusses these three elements.

A CLOSER LOOK
Kelley Brown

In a world politics course, students begin each unit by taking a pretest that asks them to respond to the unit's objectives by using four symbols: a circle for "seems interesting," a square for "might be boring," a check for "know something about," and a star for "will be challenging." From day one, students discuss and connect to the learning objectives because they know what they are. Periodically, students take out the objectives and score them on a scale of 1–3 (1 = *I don't understand this yet*, 2 = *I understand but could not give an example*, 3 = *I understand and could give a concrete example of what this means*).

In the unit "Politics of Home," one of the key objectives is that students are able to evaluate how the "loss of home" affects a person's priorities, actions, and ability to engage in politics. Students begin the unit taking the pretest using the four symbols. This helps me understand what is working and what isn't and to make modifications to help my students make connections with their learning.

During this unit, students study international migration and refugees by concentrating on the Cambodian Civil War and Genocide. I created this unit because we have a significant Cambodian population in our town and it helped me in my goal to make learning meaningful. During the unit, students select from a variety of learning materials, including videos, personal narratives, guest speakers from the community, autobiographies, and podcasts. A combination of direct instruction, simulation, interviews, reading, and research allows students to build a base of knowledge to demonstrate their understanding of the objective by either writing or creating a fictitious refugee narrative and artifact project.

Overwhelmingly, all of my students respond with interest, sincerity, and humility to this unit of study. This semester, one student remarked, "It's shocking to me that people I know had to go through this. I had no idea." When I first launched this unit, I wrongly assumed that my Cambodian students already had an understanding of what happened. They didn't. I learned that many had been born in refugee camps and knew little of the story. One such student had a rough relationship with her parents; she struggled with the pressures they put on her to succeed, and the cultural pressures were in constant conflict with other American students. She was intrigued by this unit and helped me develop the Cambodian Artifact Project. She talked to her parents about our learning. When creating her project, she narrated her "journal" to her mother, who translated it into Khmer so her father could read the journal in Khmer. One afternoon, we sat in my classroom after school discussing the unit. She said to me tearfully, "I get it now. I understand where my parents are coming from. I never knew what they went through. I know why they want me to succeed, why they impress their ideas on me." She decided to extend her learning about the objective further, and after countless hours of interviewing and editing, she developed a remarkable documentary film called *The Cambodian Community: Here in Easthampton*, which we screened for the local community. Her work taught me about the real impact that meaningful self-directed learning can have on the *whole* person.

Using the Support of the School Community to Make Learning Work

While we might think of the curriculum as what happens in the classroom, it is critical to consider the types of learning that can occur when we tap into the resources of our school and family communities as well as the community at large. Take, for example, the student in Mark's classroom who is autistic. This student's individualized education plan calls for him to participate actively in the classroom with the aid of an instructional assistant. While Mark and the instructional assistant would like the student to participate, his level of social interaction is quite distinct from that of his peers. It is helpful to draw from the school community for support in helping him engage in the types of interactions that will yield the most positive results.

An example of this type of support is the work of speech-language pathologist Maureen Penko, who works in Winnipeg, Manitoba, in Canada. She seeks ways for students to develop social skills through interacting with classmates using what Carol Gray (2010) refers to as *social stories*. Have a look to see how Maureen strengthens her student's status through these storytelling activities.

A CLOSER LOOK
Maureen Penko

The use of visual techniques is a positive way to help children develop social skills. In conversation with a Grade 3 teacher about a student "on the spectrum," she expressed that a number of students were also having difficulty with respecting personal space, making eye contact, taking turns, interrupting, and much more. We discussed that perhaps through storytelling we could develop comprehension of the importance of the appropriate behaviors, especially in the classroom. Hence the idea of using Carol Gray's social stories to develop comprehension and to establish appropriate social exchanges was launched.

As a speech-language pathologist, it is an area that I am very familiar with, so using this concept in collaboration with the teacher for the benefit of many students was an exciting one. So began the development of a series of stories titled "What Is My Body Doing," "My Talking Book," "Where Should My Eyes Be," "Sometimes I Blurt," and "Taking Turns Is Fun." The content of the stories unfolded while working with two children simultaneously. Sentence starters triggered the students' ideas, and we added graphics they created. They personalized the stories, starting with their name for authorship; added colorful detail to their specific book; underlined the important vocabulary; and added a smile at the end. The class began to look forward to hearing the books read once they were completed. The teacher suggested adding the unique books to the classroom library for other students to read. This helped with reinforcing the communication behaviors. A definite change in student self-esteem, self-worth, and importance was evidenced as fellow classmates enjoyed their books! The vocabulary, comprehension, and repetition of the appropriate behaviors lived on in the classroom as the books were read frequently. However, the aspect of self-monitoring *and social nuances* was not an easy one. So back to the drawing board to determine what learning tool to use! It struck us that we could use technology and reflect by drawing from Garcia Winner (2007) on social interaction. During the project presentations and partnership sharing, I used an iPad to record video of the students who had created the books. Later, students had a chance to view and critique with me what they saw. This aspect of self-reflection using a method of viewing oneself was so powerful that the students not only liked looking at the clip, but also selected the key words from the relevant books to identify what they were doing. Technology is so much a part of their everyday learning that using this medium was popular and allowed the students to self-regulate. We know that language and social skills are required to function in the everyday world. Effective delivery of ideas and body language can determine how we are viewed socially and in our learning environments. Helping children understand and manage their behavior is so important for developing self-regulation skills, resilience, sense of self, and social success as well as nurturing their mental health and well-being. The students experienced greater acceptance as they implemented the learning.

Drawing from the school community is essential to make learning work. It provides students with additional opportunities to interact meaningfully with others. When students support peers with different levels of expertise, it encourages students who are attempting to gain confidence to know that "if she can model it, I can imagine myself doing it." It also reinforces the sense of empowerment and capability for the student who is doing the modeling. Everybody wins. Another fine example of this in practice comes from Angela Ghent, an ESL teacher at Indian Land High School, in Lancaster County, South Carolina. Read what Angela and the school community do to care for the newest students in support of their English language development.

A CLOSER LOOK
Angela Ghent

The principal of the school, David Shamble, reaches out to these immigrants and intentionally works to make them feel like part of the school community. He looks for them at lunch to make sure they have friends to sit with. He recognizes their changes in behavior as they learn to speak more English, and he also gives them public recognition and awards for their academic achievement. He sets the tone for teachers, counselors, and administrators to give these students a warm welcome and to go the extra mile to meet their needs.

Often, teachers stop me in the hall to ask me personal questions about my students because they care. They want to know about the students, but the students can't speak English. I use a bilingual process to help students write personal narratives. Then I give the students opportunities to share their stories with the administration and teaching staff.

I scaffold the writing process by interviewing the student. The student usually communicates to me in their first language. If the student can write in their first language, we simply use Google translate. I type the question in English; the student reads it in their first language and then types the answer in their first language. I have intermediate fluency in Spanish, so if the student speaks Spanish we can have conversations. If I have other students in the room who speak a common language, I will assign the other students the task of asking questions for supporting details to expand the story. Then I model writing the story in English, which is also translated into the first language. So the student sees their story in both languages. We select key vocabulary from the story for the student to learn.

After the student's story is developed and they understand it in both languages, I give the student the opportunity to share their story with other staff members in the building. If the student has just arrived, I may simply print the story and give it to teachers that the student selects. Usually the teachers stop by to have a conversation about the story. After the student has developed some reading and speaking skills, I schedule an appointment with the principal for the student to read aloud the story in English. In order to honor the student, no knowledge of them is shared without their permission.

To borrow terms from literature class, newcomers who don't speak English have no voice. They are "flat characters" to their teachers. Newcomers who can present personal narratives to their teachers and talk about themselves through writing become "round characters." Essentially, the more we know about the lives of our students, the more we care.

Working With the Community at Large to Encourage Learning

We can and should draw from supports from the community at large. If our goal is to have interactions and lots of them, the amount of people power for accomplishing this involves our creativity in making it happen. We provide two powerful examples for thinking about how to accomplish this goal.

Ntina Paleos is a high school ESL teacher at George W. Hewlett High School in New York. In the example below, she describes a wide variety of activities that she does to ensure that ELLs are engaged in their learning process and community. Listen to Ntina's voice as she describes the activities that she uses to enlist a variety of resources to support student learning. These include cross-grade peers, alumni, and others. As you read her description, consider the ways in which Ntina engages her students to interact with her, each other, the school community, and the community at large. Ntina also discusses the importance of creating an environment that is built on mutual and authentic trust.

A CLOSER LOOK
Ntina Paleos

I would like to think of Room 108 as more than the room where ESL classes take place. I would like to think of it as a learning community that has evolved over the years to include current ELLs, exited ELLs, mainstream students, senior citizen volunteers from surrounding communities, high school seniors doing their senior projects, and the frequent visits by alumni that come and go. Chaos? No, heaven!

I knew that if I wanted students to really communicate in English, I needed to enlist the community around me to create an environment that not only required the use of English to function because of the native speaker presence, but also motivated and inspired my students to reach for language beyond the "drill and kill" sheets of traditional language acquisition. I wanted my students to want to learn English, not just for the grade, but also for the thrill of being able to communicate with their American student counterparts and other members of the school and local community.

I realized that my most valuable teaching resources were outside of Room 108. They were walking in the halls, hanging out in the cafeteria and commons area, at home, at the senior center playing mahjong, and at Burger King. Instead of venturing out into the community, I had to bring the community in! I needed to attract members of our linguistically rich community to our classroom to become members of a teaching team which would foster learning English in an authentic, meaningful way.

First, I adopted an open-door policy. This required a bit of courage on my part. I made computers available and textbooks and other resources handy to attract former students to come in. I had to find balance in teaching a class while nonregistered students would enter and exit during the course of the lesson. I finally narrowed it down to the first 10 minutes of class. Any former student who wanted to come in to use resources, tutor, contribute, audit, or just experience the fellowship of our learner community had to be there no later than 10 minutes into the period. The students that come in are often exited English-proficient students from years before who are invited back year after year. They not only help students with academics, but also serve as role models, mentoring their peers and encouraging them to work through the challenges as they did years before.

Other valuable members of our learning community are members of community organizations; many are retired teachers who come in and give their time generously to tutor and mentor our students. I have at least one volunteer in my room on any given day. They have been invited to partake in classroom presentations and multicultural parties as well. They have become our adoptive grandparents and add so much wisdom to our classroom.

Along with our adoptive grandparents, you may peek into Room 108 and find mainstream students who have signed up to teach some lessons as part of their senior project. These students intern with me for a period of time and then formulate lessons to teach for a day or two. The ELLs love to have the mainstream students teach our class! These students are often American-born who are interested in teaching one day. Having American-born students come and forge relationships with our ELL population is a step in the right direction in creating cross-cultural bridges of understanding.

Our alumni are yet another component of our learning community. These are students who have graduated high school and are invited back to give talks and encouragement to our students. Most of them come back in September as they are feeling homesick and long for the normalcy of the old friends they left behind in high school. We stay connected via Facebook, and they keep us current with what's going on in their life. They often give wonderful advice to graduating seniors and share their experiences as college freshman.

Content area teachers complete our ESL community of teachers and learners. They often stop by our classroom to watch our students present PowerPoints or recite poetry or just to say hello. During our multicultural celebrations, they are formally invited by students.

Ntina's work highlights the importance of interactions and ways for engaging a broad community in this essential process. Rather than seeing interactions as a distraction or as non-essential, she recognized them as potential opportunities for learning to happen. Following our schema of teacher-student, student-student, teacher-parent, parent-parent, teacher–school community, school community–community at large, we see a myriad of activities that Ntina routinely engages in to best ensure that her students are active and supported learners. Rather than be passive in the learning process, for example, Ntina has created an environment in which her students are comprehensively and intentionally given access to learning and support in this process. Further, she draws from her students' and their families' personal, cultural, linguistic, world, and prior academic experiences by providing them with multiple sources from which to gain this important grounding.

We might argue that Ntina's work and her situation are somehow exceptional and too hard to replicate in our own contexts (especially those of us for whom the curriculum and high-stakes tests are the driving force). Though the specifics of our situations may differ, the values that guide Ntina's choices can guide our own. Seminal research identifies a distinct correlation between a teacher's attitudes and expectations and a student's achievement and attitudes (Bamberg, 1994; Brophy, 1982). In our example, Ntina is striving for what we would want as well: a safe, secure environment that has the high expectation that her students matter. For this to happen, it is invaluable to have a learning environment characterized by unconditional and broad support.

Kristina Labadie is a G.L.A.D. language acquisition and literacy coach[3] and former fourth-grade mainstream classroom teacher in Vancouver, Washington. She understands the importance of caring for her students as well as supporting their academic growth. Recalling her experience as a fourth-grade teacher, she acknowledged the limits of her capacity to provide the volume of interactions that she knew her students needed and how she addressed this challenge. It occurred when she had a class that had "eight students on individualized education plans who were reading at first-grade reading levels as well as several others who were more than a year behind. In addition," she recounted, "the class had two students with significant behavior challenges, and more than half the class spoke a language other than English."

---

[3]According to Project G.L.A.D. (www.projectglad.com), Kristina's work involves providing professional coaching to promote English language acquisition, academic achievement, and cross-cultural skills.

A CLOSER LOOK
Kristina Labadie

A couple of years ago, I had a class with unusually high needs academically. There just wasn't enough time, or even volunteers, to go around, let alone fill the need. I have always encouraged parents to help out in the classroom either reading with students, working on math facts, or in a variety of other ways. However, this year I was not getting a lot of response and many of the families I had were in deep crisis. After the beginning-of-the-year assessments were completed, I knew I needed to think outside of the box to fill these needs.

Most of the children in my class that year were being raised by single parent moms who were incredibly young and stressed. More than half of my class had moved here from somewhere else over the prior couple years. Nearly all of my students were struggling financially or in getting their basic needs met. Two of my students would try to hide under desks or would burst into tears at the littlest things. These facts, and many others, triggered the idea that perhaps what this class needed was a set of grandparents. As a result, I sought out and convinced a retired couple I vaguely knew to begin volunteering in my school. They were rather skeptical about whether they had anything to offer, especially the husband. In addition they lived almost half an hour away. Still, I felt like they had the ability to connect with students in my class who needed them. Several of my students were English language learners, and since the wife had immigrated as a teenager I felt she could relate to what was involved in learning a language as part of school. Besides, they had the time.

This dear couple came in to my classroom twice a week and listened to students read, held conversations with students, and worked on math facts. They had no ties other than knowing me, but they brought a warm and loving personality with them. The husband was a retired engineer and extremely tall. This intimidated my rather short group of fourth graders at first; however, that didn't last and soon the students were begging to read with "that Mister." Two boys in particular really grew to like him and would specifically bring items to talk about with him that were related to the books they wanted to share. What a sight to see this giant of a man walking down the hall with one of my very, very short boys. One of my girls couldn't wait each week to talk with the wife and planned ahead to make the most of her time. One day this student told me that she absolutely needed to talk with her about something I "just wouldn't be able to understand." Turns out, my student had been getting teased about her accent at recess and she wanted ideas about what to say.

What a blessing this couple was to my class! My students even asked to invite them to our end-of-the-year party and wanted them to sign their yearbook since they considered them part of our class. However, it didn't stop there. I recently learned that this couple has kept in contact with one of the students through email. More exciting is the fact that while I have moved to a different position and it isn't realistic for the couple to volunteer for me anymore, they enjoyed their experience so much they sought out a local school and volunteered again as honorary grandparents, continuing to make a difference in the lives of students they would never have known otherwise.

REFLECTION ACTIVITIES

Time for Reflection

Reflect on the following questions and write a response.

1. List some goals and purposes you might have in increasing the amount and quality of student interactions to support learning in your classroom.

2. Describe how you might draw from the school community and community at large to broaden the amount of student interactions. Use as many details as you can to describe what you would do and how this would work.

As educators, we often have the pleasure of discovering that the students we work with thrive, sometimes as a direct result of what we tried to give them. But sadly, there are also instances when we learn of students that are facing struggles academically, with social status, psychologically, and with other significant stressors. In these situations, we ask ourselves: What could we have done to make a difference?

For example, in a presidential address to the American Education Research Association, Carol Lee (2010) described the outcome of one student accordingly: "By the time Yetu was a sophomore, he was the father of twins. By his junior year, one of his twins died, and he had been kicked out of school, suspected of selling drugs" (p. 643).

She asks herself and us: What could have been done to support Yetu to be more successful in school? This is a critical question that we should be asking ourselves as we consider what we do and why we do it. In other words, how can and should we look at the various ways in which we support our diverse group of students, especially those from underserved populations, to provide them with a sense of unconditional support as well as sound, appropriate, and useful academic experiences that will serve their growth as learners and as people?

Summary

In this chapter we considered how to use the climate of trust and community to promote the academic success of all learners. We took into consideration the curriculum standards, English language development standards for English learners, individualized education plans for students with special education, as well as a school or district's curriculum to discuss how to impart a positive message that all learners can learn, understand that all learners and families are smart and can contribute to learning, make learning socially and personally relevant, create a caring community of learners, understand the process and task elements of academic interactions, make learning visible and transparent, use the support of the school community to make learning work; and work with the community at large to encourage learning. In our next chapter, we will explore using classroom events to empower students and families.

References

Bamberg, J. D. (1994). *Raising expectations to improve student learning.* Oak Brook, IL: North Central Regional Educational Laboratory (ERIC Document Reproduction Service No. ED378290)

Board of Regents of the University of Wisconsin System. (2012). *2012 amplification of the English language development standards, kindergarten–grade 12.* Retrieved from http://www.wida.us/standards/eld.aspx

Bowlby, J. (1969). *Attachment: Vol. 1. Attachment and loss.* London, UK: Hogarth.

Brophy, J. E. (1982). *Research on the self-fulfilling prophecy and teacher expectations.* East Lansing: Michigan State University, Institute for Research on Teaching. (ERIC Document Reproductions Service No. ED221530)

Chiu, M. M. (2004). Adapting teacher interventions to student needs during cooperative learning: How to improve student problem solving and time on task. *American Educational Research Journal, 41*, 365–399.

Cohen, E. G., & Lotan, R. (2014). *Designing groupwork: Strategies for the heterogeneous classroom* (10th ed.). New York, NY: Teachers College Press.

Common Core State Standards Initiative. (2014). *Grade 2: Operations and algebraic thinking.* Retrieved from http://www.corestandards.org/Math/Content/2/OA/

Craig, S. (2008). *Teaching and reaching children who hurt: Strategies for your classroom.* Baltimore, MD: Paul H. Brookes.

Derolf, S., & Letzig, M. (2011). *The crayon box that talked.* New York, NY: Random House.

Freire, P. (1993). *Pedagogy of the oppressed.* New York, NY: Continuum.

Gray, C. (2010). *The new social story book: Over 150 social stories that teach everyday social skills to children with autism or Asperger's syndrome, and their peers* (Rev. and exp. ed.). Arlington, TX: Future Horizons.

Halliday, M. A. K. (1985). *Spoken and written language.* Oxford, UK: Oxford University Press.

Lee, C. D. (2010). Soaring above the clouds, delving the ocean's depths: Understanding the ecologies of human learning and the challenge for education science. *Educational Researcher, 39*, 643–655.

Lotan, R. (2006). Teaching teachers to build equitable classrooms. *Theory Into Practice, 45*(1), 32–39.

Nodding, N. (2005). *The challenge to care in schools: An alternative approach to education* (2nd ed.). New York, NY: Teachers College Press.

Ogbu, J. U. (1992). Understanding cultural diversity and learning. *Educational Researcher, 21*(8), 5–14, 24.

Ogbu, J. U., & Simons, H. D. (1998). Voluntary and involuntary minorities: A cultural-ecological theory of school performance with some implications for education. *Anthropology & Education Quarterly, 29*(2), 155–188.

Peregoy, S. E., & Boyle, O. F. (2008). *Reading, writing and learning in ESL: A resource book for teaching K–12 English learners* (5th ed.). New York, NY: Pearson.

Pierson, R. (2013). *Every kid needs a champion.* Retrieved from https://www.ted.com/talks/rita_pierson_every_kid_needs_a_champion

Silverstone, M., & Zacarian, D. (2013). Grade 2: Evens and odds: How many in all? In M. Gottlieb & G. Ernst-Slavit (Eds.), *Academic language in diverse classrooms: Mathematics, grades K–2: Promoting content and language learning* (pp. 129–162). Thousand Oaks, CA: Corwin.

TERC. (2008). *Investigations in number, data, and space* (2nd ed.). New York, NY: Pearson.

Tosolt, B. (2009). Middle school students' perceptions of caring teacher behaviors: Differences by minority status. *Journal of Negro Education, 78*, 405–416.

Winner, M. G. (2007). *Thinking about you thinking about me* (2nd ed). San Jose, CA: Think Social Publishing Inc.

Zacarian, D. (1996). *Learning how to teach and design curriculum for the heterogeneous class: An ethnographic study of a task-based cooperative learning group of native English and English as a second language speakers in a graduate education course* (Master's thesis). Available from ProQuest Dissertations and Theses database. (UMI No. 9639055)

Zacarian, D. (2011). *Transforming schools for English learners: A comprehensive framework for school leaders.* Thousand Oaks, CA: Corwin.

Zacarian, D. (2013). *Mastering academic language: A framework for supporting student achievement.* Thousand Oaks, CA: Corwin.

6

Using Classroom Events to Empower Students and Families

For students to get the most out of school, we need to promote a partnership between parents, community leaders, and teachers. . . . Only through partnerships can our schools keep improving and stay on the right track.

—Susan Castillo, Oregon Superintendent of Public
Instruction (2003, para. 8)

> What can we do to involve families and students as partners in ways that make them active contributors to learning as members of a school-based community?

Katherine Leighton works as an eighth-grade English teacher in an urban middle school in Mississippi. To support students in developing global awareness from multiple perspectives, her school's social studies and English departments have co-designed theme-based units of study that are based on the English language arts and history/social studies goals of the Common Core State Standards (Common Core

State Standards Initiative, 2014). In English language arts classes, students will read contemporary books about adolescents that have experienced war and civil conflict, while in social studies they will study current events in the Middle East. Katherine is reviewing the book selections that are recommended, which include *Thura's Diary: A Young Girl's Life in War-Torn Baghdad* (Al-Windawi, 2004); *We Just Want to Live Here* (Rifa'i & Ainbinder, 2003), about friendship between an Israeli and a Palestinian; and *I Am Malala: The Girl Who Stood Up for Education and Was Shot by the Taliban* (Yousafzai, 2013). An important goal of the unit of study is for students to learn global perspectives on real-world issues and develop a high level of thinking and dialogue about them from various points of view. Figure 6.1 shows what the Common Core State Standards require students to do in the areas of reading, listening, and speaking.

Figure 6.1   Common Core State Standards, Grade 8 English Language
               Arts Standards

Reading—Key Ideas and Details

Cite the textual evidence that most strongly supports an analysis of what the text says explicitly as well as inferences drawn from the text.

Determine a theme or central idea of a text and analyze its development over the course of the text, including its relationship to the characters, setting, and plot; provide an objective summary of the text.

Analyze how particular lines of dialogue or incidents in a story or drama propel the action, reveal aspects of a character, or provoke a decision.

Presentation of Knowledge and Ideas

Present claims and findings, emphasizing salient points in a focused, coherent manner with relevant evidence, sound valid reasoning, and well-chosen details; use appropriate eye contact, adequate volume, and clear pronunciation.

Integrate multimedia and visual displays into presentations to clarify information, strengthen claims and evidence, and add interest.

Adapt speech to a variety of contexts and tasks, demonstrating command of formal English when indicated or appropriate.

Giving Students a Choice

As Katherine explores the various possibilities for teaching this unit of study, one that she and her colleagues know to be important is giving students a choice in what they will do to learn. The beliefs about student choice reflect the principles of motivation that we presented in Chapter 1, drawing from Daniel Pink (2012). According to educational scholars Bean, Dunkerly-Bean, and Harper (2013), they also reflect the policies of the International Reading Association, the National Council of Teachers of English, and the National Reading Conference. With this in mind, Katherine decides to separate her class into small teams that will each choose a book from the suggested list. She begins to design lesson plans for having them present the knowledge and ideas that they gain from this collaborative activity. One means for doing this, she considers, is a classroom event in which students will provide presentations about what they have learned to their families. Katherine begins to think about the possibilities for this type of event.

Why Do This?

One thing is true in all satisfying partnerships: They begin with choice and with an enthusiasm about freely chosen mutual goals. For this reason, we are especially sensitive to present information about constructing classroom and school-based events not as another responsibility that heavily burdened teachers *should* meet (that list is quite long enough) but as something we can choose to do—and others have done—to bring a transformative experience to our collective work for everyone involved. While the advantages of school efforts to integrate students and families as partners are well documented, the reality is that it may be easy for the involved and well resourced—the usual suspects—to reap the benefits of classroom and school-based events, while those who are challenged, according to Delpit (2006), Epstein et al. (2009), and Henderson, Mapp, Johnson, and Davies (2007), remain on the outside, further distanced by the obstacles to their participation. Just as we adjust our teaching practice to the unique qualities and needs of our students, we need to show a similar responsiveness to encourage and support all students and families in accessing and taking advantage of classroom and school event opportunities.

In this chapter, we offer a rationale for creating events that engage all students and families. We also discuss the importance of drawing on the experiences and cultural resources of families in this process. As in prior chapters, we provide a variety of examples to illustrate the key ideas.

Understanding the Importance of Partnerships

Welcoming students and families into the classroom and school on a more frequent basis than conventional events, such as open houses and parent conferences, brings enormous potential benefits. However, figuring out what is needed for this to occur successfully is important. Let's look at our focal teacher, Katherine. While she and her students are part of a single classroom community, they are also members of a larger group—their school community. For example, on any given day, Title 1 mathematics and English support, English as a second language (ESL), and special education staff come to Katherine's class to work with select students or students leave her class to receive these supports or instruction from them. Further, all of her students participate in activities that involve the school's physical education, art, music, guidance, and library staff and others, including school administrators. In a real sense, those who work with and on behalf of students are all members of a school community.

The school community is the sphere of influence that we highlight in this chapter to describe and illustrate the importance of classroom-based events. We also focus more closely on increasing students' learning and engagement in their classroom learning community by showing how classroom-based events can engage all families, especially those who might not typically be involved with the school. Before we begin our discussion, we want to emphasize the importance of teacher collaboration with the school community (including administrators, fellow teachers, support staff, parents, and other stakeholders). We show how these partnerships are critical for making classroom events a successful enterprise.

In earlier chapters of this book, we provided a rationale for understanding students and families as having rich resources and assets and the importance of connecting the curriculum with students' and families' personal, social, cultural, and world experiences. While these classroom and home-classroom connections are important to consider, so are partnerships with the school community. Classroom events, by their very nature, are designed and delivered for the purpose of bringing students and, at times, their families together. The events, in and of themselves, can and do require a good deal of support to ensure that everyone has rich opportunities for interaction. As such, it's important to consider the need to gain the support of our colleagues in strengthening these events' chances for success.

Let's take a closer look at the example that we presented at the opening of this chapter to illustrate the importance of involving the school community in classroom events. Katherine Leighton is going to hold a classroom event where students will present various perspectives about what they learned with their families. How might she make this event more successful by soliciting help/support from her students, colleagues, family, and even community members to co-plan and deliver the event with her as opposed to her doing it on her own? Before we respond to this question, let's look at the students in her class.

Almost all 30 of the students live in households with income below the poverty line and receive free or reduced lunch. Five of the students have identified special education needs: a student who is deaf and requires an interpreter, a student who is on the autism spectrum and learns with a full-time aide, and three who receive support from a special educator to meet their auditory processing needs. There are also 6 English learners; 3 speak Spanish, 1 speaks Arabic, 1 speaks Gujarati, and 1 speaks Japanese. Some of the English learners have school-matched language skills in their home languages, while others do not possess the grade-level school-matched academic language skills that are needed to be successful in school. Further, there are a few students who live in homeless shelters.

REFLECTION ACTIVITIES

Time for Reflection

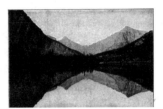

Reflect on the following questions and write a response.

1. What barriers to parent participation have you experienced in your school? (If you are not currently working in a school setting, based on your prior experience in a school setting, what barriers to parent participation did you note?)

2. Based on your response, discuss two or three remedies that Katherine might use to better ensure that the classroom event is successful.

Partnerships and Classroom-Based Events

Classroom-based events are not an end in themselves, but rather a powerful means to partially answer this crucial question: *What can I do to better involve students and families?*

When we go beyond the required open houses and seasonal parent conferences and invite families into the classroom for events that we create, it has the potential of sending many powerful messages to them:

- We are interested in knowing you.
- We value your participation.
- Our classroom is a community, and there's a place for you in it as we work together out of a shared caring about your son or daughter.
- We think it's important that you have the chance to know us.
- We're comfortable with your questions and your involvement.

When adults are invited in to share student successes or participate in them, it can also convey messages to our students:

- Families and teachers are working together on your behalf because they care about you.
- We are proud and excited about the work of each and every one of you, and we want to share it with families.
- Our learning is a source of interest, celebration, and pride for us as well as our families.

To realize this potential of these events requires that we consider them as a means for collaborating and working together. An important first step in planning events is to review the calendar.

Understanding the School Year Calendar to Plan for Optimal Involvement

Regardless of where we work, we operate according to the school calendar that has been created for our institution. When we did a Google search of the phrase "school calendar," we received over 900 million results! The first calendar on the search list, at the time that we performed this task, was from Anchorage, Alaska. We have copied it here (Figure 6.2) for the purpose of understanding how to work with our school schedules to plan for optimal events.

While each school or district's calendar may look slightly different, they always provide a snapshot of the academic schedule. For example,

Figure 6.2   2014–2015 Anchorage, Alaska, School Year Calendar

Anchorage School District

2014 – 15 School Year Calendar*

S	M	T	W	T	F	S
			July			
		1	2	3	4	5
6	7	8	9	10	11	12
13	14	15	16	17	18	19
20	21	22	23	24	25	26
27	28	29	30	31		

S	M	T	W	T	F	S
			August			
					1	2
3	4	5	6	7	8	9
10	11	12	13	**14**	15	16
17	18	19	(20	21	22	23
24	25	26	K-1	28	29	30
31						

S	M	T	W	T	F	S
			September			
	1	2	3	4	5	6
7	8	9	10	11	12	13
14	15	16	17	18	19	20
21	22	23	24	25	26	27
28	29	30				

S	M	T	W	T	F	S
			October			
			1	2	3	4
5	6	7	8	9	10	11
12	13	14	15	16	17)	18
19	(20	21	22	23	24	25
26	27	28	29	30	31	

S	M	T	W	T	F	S
			November			
						1
2	3	4	5	6	7	8
9	10	11	12	13	14	15
16	17	18	19	20	21	22
23	24	25	26	27	28	29
30						

S	M	T	W	T	F	S
			December			
	1	2	3	4	5	6
7	8	9	10	11	12	13
14	15	16	17	18	19)	20
21	22	23	24	25	26	27
28	29	30	31			

AUGUST
14 Teachers' first day
15 18 19 State released professional development day**
20 Classes begin
K-1 27 Classes begin for K-1

SEPTEMBER
1 Labor Day holiday**

OCTOBER
17 State released professional development day. End of first quarter**
22 23 Parent conference days. School schedules and student-release times vary. Check with your school for specific schedule.
24 State released professional development day.**

NOVEMBER
27-28 Thanksgiving holiday**

DECEMBER
19 State released grade reporting day. End of second quarter**
22-31 Winter break**

JANUARY
1-2 Winter break** (cont.)
19 Martin Luther King Jr. holiday**

FEBRUARY
16 Presidents Day holiday**
18 19 Parent conference days. School schedules and student-release times vary. Check with your school for specific schedule.
20 State released professional development day.**

MARCH
6 State released grade reporting day. End of third quarter**
9-13 Spring Break**
3/30-5/1 AMP (Alaska Measures of Progress) state testing window
  March 30-April 10: grades 3 and 7
  April 6-17: grades 4 and 8
  April 13-24: grades 5 and 9
  April 20-May 1: grades 6 and 10

MAY
21 Classes end, end of fourth quarter
22 Teachers' last day.
25 Memorial Day holiday

( ) Beginning, end of quarter

S	M	T	W	T	F	S
			January			
				1	2	3
4	(5	6	7	8	9	10
11	12	13	14	15	16	17
18	19	20	21	22	23	24
25	26	27	28	29	30	31

S	M	T	W	T	F	S
			February			
1	2	3	4	5	6	7
8	9	10	11	12	13	14
15	16	17	(18)	(19)	20	21
22	23	24	25	26	27	28

S	M	T	W	T	F	S
			March			
1	2	3	4	5	6)	7
8	9	10	11	12	13	14
15	(16	17	18	19	20	21
22	23	24	25	26	27	28
29	30	31				

S	M	T	W	T	F	S
			April			
			1	2	3	4
5	6	7	8	9	10	11
12	13	14	15	16	17	18
19	20	21	22	23	24	25
26	27	28	29	30		

S	M	T	W	T	F	S
			May			
					1	2
3	4	5	6	7	8	9
10	11	12	13	14	15	16
17	18	19	20	21)	22	23
24	25	26	27	28	29	30
31						

S	M	T	W	T	F	S
			June			
	1	2	3	4	5	6
7	8	9	10	11	12	13
14	15	16	17	18	19	20
21	22	23	24	25	26	27
28	29	30				

* subject to change   ** students do not attend school   07-24-14

Source: Anchorage Public Schools (2014).

in Anchorage, the school year begins in August, and in October, students take the state exam and parent conferences are held. Taking the calendar into account is essential for three important reasons:

1. It requires that we follow a particular schedule, which shapes the pacing of instruction and learning and the timing and duration of units of study.

2. It specifies dates for routine events.

3. Most important for our current purposes, it provides a means for determining an optimal schedule for classroom events that are most likely to yield the best outcome, the greatest complement to classroom studies, and the best possibilities for direct family participation.

In addition to the school calendar, it is also critical to become familiar with the dates of the religious holidays of our diverse communities and events that community members are likely to be involved in (e.g., elections, other local events). For example, in the fall, there are Jewish holidays that might conflict with a classroom or school event. There are also Muslim holidays, such as Ramadan, a fasting holiday that may conflict with an event that involves food.

Our focal teacher, Katherine, meets with colleagues to discuss the date for her classroom event. At their initial meeting, they bring the school calendar and use their handheld devices to secure information about various holidays and other events so they can brainstorm optimal date possibilities for the classroom event.

Types of Classroom-Based Events

There is an array of forms that a classroom-based event can take. These fall broadly into four categories with each having a different purpose:

- community-building events for social purposes
- showcasing curriculum to make learning transparent
- drawing on the rich resources of families
- building a home/school shared culture of learning: engaging and supporting parents

Community-Building Events for Social Purposes

In a school year, early actions can mean the difference between establishing a positive tone or continually having to react to problems and attempting to catch up. When we make early efforts to reach out to families and make contact with school as comfortable and convenient as possible, it can set a tone for family communities and ourselves. It can counter expectations that some families may have of schools as intimidating or unwelcoming places. It can also bring to light new understandings about our student and family communities that we might not otherwise have. When families feel a sense of being included in the life of the classroom, they are more likely to have an attitude of cooperation and respect toward their child's educators, which can often influence students to make stronger commitments and exercise greater persistence in classroom work (Hughes & Kwok, 2007). The same might be said for us. When we feel a sense of partnership with families, we are more likely to have an attitude of cooperation and respect for them.

Events that invite families into our classrooms and bring them together for a social purpose—especially when held before the standard open house or parent conferences—can create powerful momentum for positive relationships in the year ahead. At Katherine's middle school, for example, her team of colleagues (including mathematics, social studies, and science teachers; specialists; support staff; and a school administrator) hold an opening-of-the-year Family Picnic during the first week of school. During the event, families and staff bring their own dinner and enjoy the time with each other.

The purpose of a social event is to invite everyone together in celebration of students and each other. We use the word *invite* because it is a request that we are making for families to participate in doing something with us. As we discussed earlier in this book, we believe it is critical to engage families in social events that match their personal, social, and cultural experiences. The efforts to do this could include the following:

- collaboratively planning an event to be welcoming and social
- being positive and proactive to bring family communities together
- translating notices into the languages of students' families
- considering ways to reach families who may not have email or phone service
- finding parents or guardians willing to personally invite others who may need encouragement or help to get to the school
- having "greeters," including newcomers, give out name tags, engage families in conversation, and connect with those who may be attending school events for the first time
- including translators who are members of the various communities of our students' families

While this may at first seem like a lot of effort for a simple social event, it can have a powerful influence throughout the school year in opening channels of communication and involvement that extend way beyond this context. Bringing families face to face with each other, for example, opens new possibilities for partnerships. As a parent once said, "It made me a little braver to come into school when another mother called me." Also, once an event like this breaks the ice, it becomes much more easy and imaginable to do it again and again and/or connect directly with families in other ways.

REFLECTION ACTIVITIES

Time for Reflection

Reflect on the following questions and write a response.

1. Consider the goals and objectives for holding a social event. What activities might you plan in your particular context?

2. Based on what you have written, who would you partner with to make it work?

It is important to consider the differences among our students' family communities in terms of those who represent dominant U.S. culture in which independence and competition are highly valued versus families who represent cultures with a more collectivist belief system in which group harmony and relationships are highly valued (DeCapua

& Marshall, 2011; Hofstede, 2001; Hofstede & Hofstede, 2005). We presented a fuller discussion of this in Chapter 2, but we reference it here to emphasize the importance of building foundational social relationships with families to match many of the cultural groups with whom we work.

The goal behind these early events is to build from a social foundation of relationships. And as we learn about our students and their families' cultures and personal situations, we are better able to anticipate how to best support their active participation in school life and, possibly, infuse cultural events into our classrooms to affirm these student and family communities.

Showcasing Curriculum to Make Learning Transparent

Curriculum-centered events held at times that are convenient for families, and that consider the supports and encouragements they need, can increase the potential of families to powerfully advance the academic engagement of our students. These might include *achievement recognitions,* such as those for reading or publication celebrations for student writing, as well as poetry slams and debates about curriculum topics that students have studied. Such events allow families to see and even participate, firsthand, in what students are learning.

These kinds of events show students that what they are doing is validated by attention from beyond the classroom and that school and family stand together behind them, normalizing the idea that home and school are connected and that the demands of school are intended to be for their benefit rather than hostile. They also give parents a way to see their sons and daughters in their best light and to better understand, take pride in, and feel a part of the content of what students are learning. Even for the adults who can't actually attend, the events send the powerful and constructive message that school is a place that makes the effort to reach out to them in considerate ways in a partnership that supports students. Any elective actions done out of a willingness to create community and lower barriers to participation is trust building. For example, when a teacher translates invitation notices, personally contacts parents who may not be able to attend in person to be informed and encourage them, or connects families with transportation or other resources, it says: *Your child's school cares about you as a partner in their learning.*

It's important to acknowledge, however, that communities differ in their ability to support events at school. After-hours safety may be an issue, as are the different degrees of accessibility of buildings before and after school hours for reasons outside teachers' control. Still, there are ways to reach out to families to involve them meaningfully in their children's studies that do involve events at school. All such actions have the potential to generate trust and to have lasting power and use-fulness during the course of a school year and students' careers; they may also lay the groundwork for future communication, cooperation, and information sharing. Indeed, this type of sharing can be essential to the success of students who may need a boost. Families can provide teachers with crucial insights that might never come to light otherwise. This reality amplifies the importance of understanding, valuing, and drawing from the diverse resources of students' family communities. Let's look at two teachers to provide examples of this in practice.

Alexandra McCourt and Sylvia Schumann are ESL teachers in an elementary school in East Hampton, New York. They highlight the positive influences that can occur when we collaborate with families, the school community, and the community at large. Let's have a look at how their students, whom they refer to as *ESL students*, share what they have learned with various members of their community. Alexandra and Sylvia begin this discussion by sharing the challenges that their students typically experience.

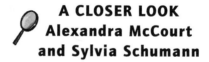

A CLOSER LOOK
Alexandra McCourt
and Sylvia Schumann

One of the greatest challenges for ESL students is adapting to and fitting into their new community, while at the same time keeping ties to their own culture. There is often a divide between the English-speaking and non-English-speaking communities. In order to bridge that divide and get the students to more fully interact with the community, the ESL department designs instruction and learning, not just for the academic needs of the students, but as a venue to spread knowledge about both the students' native cultures and the school community culture as well.

During Hispanic Heritage Month our third-grade ESL students focused on researching and writing biographies on important Hispanics from every country and region represented in our school community. Students researched and discussed the influential contributions of Hispanics from an assortment of positions in society all over the world. Students then created biography posters displaying the various country names and flags as well as the important contributions each featured person has made in the world.

The students then practiced and presented the biographies at our All School Meeting program, which occurs on alternate Friday mornings, where the entire school community, parents, and guests from the outside community are invited.

The biography presentation was prefaced by a display of Spanish words that have been adopted into the English language and a quick speech about the importance of maintaining native languages and cultures. Spanish speakers in the audience were directly addressed and encouraged to participate in the school community. The third-grade ESL students then presented the biographies with pride and later displayed them prominently in the school hallway for all community members to view.

Directly after the presentation, parents and community members alike approached both students and the ESL teachers to commend them on the celebration and incorporation of the vast array of Hispanic countries and cultures represented at the All School Meeting. Hispanic community members acknowledged their sense of pride and delight in having important persons from their own countries represented. Additionally, English-speaking parents and community members mentioned how they were struck by the numerous contributions that Hispanics have made in our society. During discussions with parents and community members, the ESL teachers invited the entire community to participate in the school's International Heritage Fair, where all the cultures of the school community are celebrated through music, dancing, guest speakers, informational pamphlets, and food.

Alexandra and Sylvia encourage this kind of sharing throughout the school year so that their students can continuously engage peers, families, and the school community in this process. Their CultureGram activity exemplifies this type of engagement.

On a monthly basis we incorporate facts about featured cultures ("CultureGrams") from our school community. We ask students to talk with their family members and members of the community to share, celebrate, and embrace customs and traditions from around the world. While our students and their families may face challenges in adjusting and acclimating to their new culture and community, our hope is to keep working toward connecting everyone in the school and the entire extended community together as a whole.

Let's revisit Katherine, the middle school English language arts teacher that we introduced at the beginning of this chapter. She collaborated with various school community members, including the deaf educator, ESL staff, and special education staff who work with her students. They want to participate in the classroom event that she is planning. She also asked the school's outreach worker to help her invite families to the event. She, too, has agreed to help Katherine at the event. With all of this support, each of the five student teams selected a book from the choices that Katherine offered and created a 15-minute presentation about it for their families. One group created a play. Another designed a poster presentation. In the third group, each student planned to read a sentence from the book and explain why it was meaningful. The fourth group wrote poetry. And the fifth group wrote a song.

REFLECTION ACTIVITIES

Time for Reflection

Considering the event that Katherine has created:

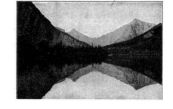

1. Discuss two or three strengths that you feel it has.

2. Discuss two areas that might need her attention to better ensure success.

Drawing on the Rich Resources of Families

Families from diverse personal, social, cultural, linguistic, and socioeconomic backgrounds can bring a wide range of resources and experiences to our classrooms. These can greatly help to support content and literacy learning and give all of our students a greater understanding of our global society (Gonzalez, McIntyre, & Rosebury, 2001; Gonzalez, Moll, & Amanti, 2005). We can affirm and support families and, most important, our students' learning and membership in their learning community by recognizing and tapping into the rich resources of families. These can take a variety of forms, including but not limited to the following:

Personal/career connection to learning and community. This might be a soldier returning from Afghanistan who is invited to discuss her personal experiences with members of the Afghani community. Or an entomologist who is invited to present a discussion on butterflies when his child's class is studying the life cycle and migration patterns of Monarch butterflies.

Cultural/linguistic connection to learning and community. An example of this might be the veteran parent who is a member of particular group, such as a Spanish-speaking mother from a small town in Ecuador. She might be called on to support a new family from the same Ecuadoran community. Additionally, it can include the parent who is invited to class to share a folk story, type of food, or song that is indigenous to his culture in connection to a topic that is being studied or is part of a community-building activity.

World experience connection to learning and community. This might include the parent who is invited to the classroom to discuss her immigration experience when her child's class is studying this topic in U.S. history.

Social connection to learning and community. These can involve parents or grandparents coming to the classroom to read to students or listen to students read. Some additional possibilities are playing a board game, teaching dance, or sharing craft project skills with students to give them meaningful hands-on learning extensions for the learning objectives being explored in class.

REFLECTION ACTIVITIES
Time for Reflection

Reflect on the following question and write a response.

Discuss two or three additional activities that draw from families' world and/or social experiences.

Building a Home/School Shared Culture of Learning: Engaging and Supporting Parents

It is important to consider how our classrooms can support families in their children's achievement. While all children can benefit from support, factors such as language barriers or lack of school-based information (ranging from what typically occurs in school to post–high school planning) disadvantage families who don't have firsthand experience in navigating this territory themselves (Rowan-Kenyon, Bell, & Perna, 2008). For this reason schools have an opportunity to build scaffolding that helps students with fewer resources reach the places that students from families with higher socioeconomic status start out from.

Family curriculum events are a means to make the instructional activities that occur in class more familiar. They can also support families to be in a better position to directly support, or better understand, what their children are learning. An example is the third-grade teacher who wants to support his students in practicing their multiplication facts. This occurred in response to parent requests for more information about how to help their children at home. Families were invited to his class to see and perform the kinds of math multiplication problems that students were learning to solve in his class. As stated previously, these events can be made more successful when we are sure to schedule them during times when families are available. It is also important to work with the school community to remedy various obstacles that might get in the way of these events (e.g., need for child care, translation). The support of administrators, colleagues, guidance, and support staff can help to make what seems impossible possible. For example, our focal teacher, Katherine Leighton, enlisted the support of her colleagues to help figure out who could provide child care during her classroom event. A group of students from another team, with guided support of one of the school administrators, provided child care.

Building Student-to-Student Community

Though events may appear to be "for" families, the incidental benefits of preparing for them give students a motivation and a context for rising to the occasion with a sense of purpose. In the case of a student performance or showcase of work, the shared goal of wanting a successful presentation or event can amplify the benefits of cooperation and partnerships and bring out the best in our students. Let's take a closer look at what two teachers shared about students working together.

Third-grade teacher. During the rehearsals and performances of our play about the life and work of Dr. Martin Luther King Jr., my class was at its best—patient with each other during rehearsals, tolerant of the fluency struggles that a classmate might have with reading a line, and so proud when the whole group did such a great job for the families. It was my class at its best. I remember wondering, "Where did these children come from?" They had been here the whole time, just needing an opportunity to show it.

Ninth-grade English teacher. For our family stories project, we took a risk and intentionally paired students who have shown very different levels of school performance and who might not otherwise have chosen to socialize or work together. That's what made this presentation so powerful. Because students knew families would be seeing what they did, they pulled together to show their best side and help each other succeed. In the process they really went beyond what they might do in terms of rising to the occasion, being their best and helping their partner be at their best in front of their special audience.

REFLECTION ACTIVITIES

Time for Reflection

Reflect on the following questions and write a response.

1. What messages and impressions about your classroom community might you hope to send to students and families in the early stages of a school year? What are some ways that you could demonstrate those messages with actions?

(Continued)

(Continued)

2. What benefits do you imagine would result from having family-inclusive events in school?

3. Imagine an event that you might undertake that includes families. Describe it and brainstorm ways that you might be able to use the occasion to promote constructive relationships in these areas:

- student-to-student interactions
- family-to-family interactions
- family-to-teacher and teacher-to-family interactions
- classroom-to-community interactions

Summary

Research shows that increasing opportunities for family involvement and engagement improves learning outcomes across different demographic groups. However, proactive steps are necessary to ensure that the divide that separates the most challenged students and families are not inadvertently reinforced by the invisible barriers to their full participation. Efforts to involve families can be part of a campaign that we undertake to promote a positive tone of constructive partnership among families, students, and teachers. If done properly, students and families may feel a sense of community membership that has a positive influence on trust, attitudes, and the work of the classroom in general.

In the next chapter, we will explore our final sphere of influence, the community at large, to explore a critical element: learning through community service.

References

Al-Windawi, T. (2004). *Thura's diary: A young girl's life in war-torn Baghdad.* New York, NY: Viking.

Anchorage Public Schools. (2014). *Anchorage School District: 2014–15 school year calendar.* Retrieved from https://www.asdk12.org/media/anchorage/globalmedia/documents/calendar/2014_15.pdf

Bean, T. W., Dunkerly-Bean, J., & Harper, H. J. (2013). *Teaching young adult literature: Developing students as world citizens.* Thousand Oaks, CA: Sage.

Castillo, S. (2003, June 12). The need for partnership between schools and communities is exemplified in Knappa, Astoria. *Daily Astorian.* Retrieved from http://www.dailyastorian.com

Common Core State Standards Initiative. (2014). *English language arts standards: Anchor standards: College and career readiness anchor standards for speaking and listening.* Retrieved from http://www.corestandards.org/ELA-Literacy/CCRA/SL

DeCapua, A., & Marshall, H. W. (2011). *Breaking new ground: Teaching students with limited or interrupted formal education in U.S. secondary schools.* Ann Arbor: University of Michigan Press.

Delpit, L. (2006). *Other people's children: Cultural conflict in the classroom* (3rd ed.). New York, NY: W. W. Norton.

Epstein, J., Sanders, M. G., Sheldon, S. B., Simon, B. S., Salinas, K. C., Rodriguez Jansorn, N. R., . . . Williams, K. J. (2009). *School, family, and community partnerships: Your handbook for action* (3rd ed.). Thousand Oaks, CA: Corwin.

Gonzalez, N., McIntyre, E., & Rosebury, A. S. (Eds.). (2001). *Classroom diversity: Connecting curriculum to students' lives.* Portsmouth, NH: Heinemann.

Gonzalez, M., Moll, L. C., & Amanti, C. (2005). *Funds of knowledge: Theorizing practices in households, communities, and classrooms.* Mahwah, NJ: Lawrence Erlbaum.

Henderson, A., Mapp, K., Johnson, V., & Davies, D. (2007). *Beyond the bake sale: The essential guide to family-school partnerships.* New York, NY: New Press.

Hofstede, G. (2001). *Culture's consequences: Comparing values, behaviors, institutions, and organizations across nations* (2nd ed.). Thousand Oaks, CA: Sage.

Hofstede, G., & Hofstede, G. J. (2005). *Cultures and organizations: Software of the mind* (2nd ed.). New York, NY: McGraw-Hill.

Hughes, J., & Kwok, O. (2007). Influence of student-teacher and parent-teacher relationships on lower achieving readers' engagement and achievement in the primary grades. *Journal of Educational Psychology, 99*(1), 39–51.

Pink, D. (2012). *To sell is human: The surprising truth about moving others.* New York, NY: Riverhead Books.

Rifa'i, A., & Ainbinder, O. (2003). *We just want to live here.* New York, NY: St. Martin's.

Rowan-Kenyon, H. T., Bell, A. D., & Perna, L. W. (2008). Contextual influences on parental involvement in college going: Variations by socioeconomic class. *Journal of Higher Education, 79,* 564–586.

Yousafzai, M. (with Lamb, C.). (2013). *I am Malala: The girl who stood up for education and was shot by the Taliban.* London, UK: Weidenfeld & Nicolson.

7

Widening the Circle Beyond the Classroom

Service Learning

When I write something for my teacher, it is pretty much just for me. When we did an interview project with seniors, we learned a lot but it's for them too. It was real, we weren't just writing another paper, but someone's history, so we had to get it right.

—Fifth-Grade Student

Student participation in high-quality service learning is positively related to gains in the following key outcomes at statistically significant levels:

- *Academic engagement*
- *Educational aspirations*
- *Acquisition of 21st century skills*
- *Community engagement*

—Education Commission of the States (2014)

What are some ways students can contribute to the welfare of others beyond their classroom while also deepening their engagement with learning?

There are many examples of students learning in the service of others. Here are two examples that show the connection of learning to the world beyond the classroom. The first occurred in Montpelier, VT, and the second in Los Angeles, CA.

After overheating on a hot day during recess at the beginning of a school year, Kindergarten students in Montpelier, Vermont, identified the lack of shade trees in their playground to be a problem for the whole school. They enlisted the help of parents, local businesses, and town officials to help bring about their plan of planting shade trees in the schoolyard. In the process, they also learned about the life cycle and growing needs of trees (KIDS Consortium, 2011).

In Los Angeles, 12th graders saw a need to increase citizen participation on issues affecting their school and their city. They organized and conducted a voter registration drive partnering with the League of Women Voters and the Los Angeles County Registrar of Voters. In the process, they organized an informational assembly for students, advertising and canvassing campaigns, and they worked at polling stations (Los Angeles Unified School District, n.d.).

Why Is Service Learning Critical?

Throughout our book, we have highlighted ways in which we can draw on the diverse perspectives, energy, and shared interests of students, families, colleagues, and others by cultivating partnerships and inviting engagement. Few motivators may be more powerful to learners than the opportunity to offer useful service to others. As a learning method, it gives students the opportunity to have direct and practical real-world encounters with the concepts and ideas that they are studying. The National Youth Leadership Council (n.d.-b) defines this type of learning as "an approach to teaching and learning in which students use academic knowledge and skills to address genuine community needs." We believe that it also offers dimensions of understanding that are not possible in classrooms alone and that partnerships are critical for these benefits to occur.

It is this sphere of influence, building partnerships and working with the community at large, that we focus on in this chapter. We begin with a short summary of service learning in public education. We then highlight the inequities of access to it that are occurring in contemporary education.

Tracing the Historical Roots of Service Learning

While its modern origins can be traced back a hundred years or more to the educational theories of U.S. psychologist and educational thinker John Dewey and, more recently, to the 1970s to Brazilian educator Paolo Freire (Giles & Eyler, 1994), service learning became a widely recognized practice with the signing of the National Community and Service Act by President George H. W. Bush in 1990 and the National Community and Service Trust Act by President Bill Clinton in 1993. The two initiatives ushered in a growth era of service learning as schools became eligible to apply for federal funds to support this work. Federally funded studies show that, by 1999, 32% of the nation's public schools were sponsoring service learning projects; by 2011, almost every state had developed legislation or state board of education policies that actively promoted service learning and provided guidance about standards for its implementation (Ryan, 2012).

Service Learning as an Equity Issue

Though service learning was enacted nationally and broadly, it has been significantly hampered since 2011 by the curtailment of federal funding. While some states continue to support it with state financial support, it primarily occurs in districts that have already established it as a practice and in middle- and high-income areas (Ryan, 2012). Districts located in low-income areas have seen a broad decline in this critical component of a child's education. One of the key reasons for the decline is that it is seen as an unaffordable luxury or supplement to what is key, as opposed to a vital aspect of learning. Budget constraints and the push for high-stakes test readiness have also taken a toll on service learning (Ryan, 2012; Spring & Grimm, 2008).

This is especially unfortunate because the need for learning experiences that connect students to their local, state, national, and even global communities and a meaningful purpose is greater than ever. Evidence of this can be seen in the Guilford County, North Carolina, schools. Guilford County made a commitment to widespread implementation of service learning in 2008. By the end of the 2011–2012 school year, with 72,000 students enrolled in 124 schools, it saw a significant decrease in suspensions as well as a significant rise in graduation rates, college scholarships, and standardized test scores, and school performance (National Youth Leadership Council, n.d.-a). Improvements like these exemplify why service learning is such a powerful means for improving schools and, most important, students' performance in school and beyond.

While the federal actions helped to greatly expand its popularity, the most valuable element in service learning implementation is educators who are willing to make alliances or partnerships with community partners and engage their students in real-world activities. This can be done on levels large and small. In addition, these are just the sorts of projects that attract underwriting and support from community partners when a classroom or school community reaches out to them.

Developers of the Common Core State Standards point to the need for "deeper learning" strategies in order to help students meet Common Core curriculum expectations. The National Center for Learning and Citizenship cited service learning as a means to develop important skills (e.g., higher order thinking, synthesizing of ideas) in a meaningful context. Further, it recognized the qualities of service learning as helping to give context to skills in the following areas:

- basic skills in reading and math
- critical thinking skills
- knowledge of the economic system
- global awareness
- civic engagement
- collaborative group skills
- productivity and self-efficacy
- information and communications technology literacy
- creativity and innovation (Guilfoyle & Ryan, 2013)

Another powerful benefit of service learning is that it infuses purpose and engagement into the lives of young people. Although many think that it is too costly or takes students out of the classroom too much (especially because of the assumption that more time in class leads to better test outcomes), service learning is a powerful and proven method that should be a part of every school and district—rich and poor. The downside of not including service learning opportunities is highlighted in renowned educational visionary and reformer Ted Sizer's (1984) book *Horace's Compromise: The Dilemma of the American High School*. The book was published more than 30 years ago, but his findings are just as relevant today as they were then. Sizer asks readers to picture themselves as students in public schools and then describes the conditions that most students experience. These are likely to be familiar to nearly every public school student, particularly those in middle and high schools:

> to change subjects abruptly every hour, to be talked at incessantly, to be asked to sit still for long periods, to be endlessly tested and measured against others, to be moved around in cohorts by people who really do not know who you are, to be

denied any civility like a coffee break and asked to eat lunch in twenty-three minutes, to be rarely trusted, and to repeat the same regimen with virtually no variation for week after week, year after year. (Sizer, 1984, p. xi)

Improving learning outcomes it is not merely a matter of making learning more interactive among students. As humans, our natural drive to make a meaningful contribution to a community or to the larger world is profoundly engaging and motivating. Studies of adult motivation reveal that when workers are able to see how their efforts make a positive difference in the lives of others, they become more productive and effective in their tasks. For example, a study of lifeguards who learned about how other lifeguards rescued drowning swimmers showed a 43% increase in hours worked and 21% improvement in the safety evaluations of lifeguard supervisors (Grant, 2008). In another study, radiologists who saw a photo of a patient were documented as having written longer detailed reports and showing greater diagnostic accuracy (Grant & Parker, 2009; Turner, Hadas-Halperin, & Raveh, 2008). When we consider school as a student's workplace and learning as work, we can apply the same logic. We can also apply the ideas of guided mentorships here in terms of helping students apprentice into the workplace. It is reasonable, therefore, to expect that students' motivation to make a meaningful contribution creates greater and deeper potential for intrinsic motivation than grades or scores can alone.

Service Learning for Promoting Democratic Principles

If we look closely at the founding principles of U.S. public schools, we see the critical importance of this method. Public schools were founded, in part, with the intent of advancing citizenship. This key purpose is detailed in the National Standards for Civics and Government (Center for Civic Education, 1994), which describe the goal of K–12 schools as "developing competent and responsible citizens who possess a reasoned commitment to the fundamental values and principles that are essential to the preservation and improvement of U.S. constitutional democracy (abstract)." The same document provides additional details about the goals of these citizenship standards.

By the year 2000, all students will leave grades 4, 8, and 12 having demonstrated competency over challenging subject matter including . . . civics and government . . . so that they may be prepared for responsible citizenship, further learning, and productive employment. . . . All students will be involved in activities that promote and demonstrate . . . good citizenship, community service, and personal responsibility. (Center for Civic Education, 1994 p. 7)

In this chapter, we consider how educators have used service learning to advance both academic and civic education goals. We also show how our interactive sphere of influence (between and among teachers, students, families, the school community, and the community at large) provides a wealth of opportunities for students to interact in the service of their civic and global communities.

REFLECTION ACTIVITIES

Time for Reflection

Reflect on the following questions and write a response.

1. Imagine you were going to try to make a convincing presentation about a specific service learning project to colleagues on your team. Create the 30-second "elevator pitch" you might use to garner your team's support.

2. Write an "email" to an administrator or community partner in which you seek her or his support for this same service learning project (or a different one). List at least three concerns you would most want to address to have this person back your efforts.

Framework for Service Learning

At the state, regional, and national levels, organizations such as the Youth Innovation Fund, Learn and Serve America, the National Youth Leadership Council, Youth Service America, the KIDS Consortium, RCM Research Corporation, and the Education Commission of the States have developed guidelines, standards, and suggested protocols for teachers to develop successful service learning projects. To support the development of academically focused and purposeful service, they have developed or adopted seven standards that are widely recognized as essential elements of successful programs:

1. Meeting a recognized need in the community

2. Achieving curricular objectives through service learning—allowing classroom knowledge to be applied and tested in real life settings

3. Engaging in reflection activities in the form of discussions, journaling, performing, writing, etc.

4. Developing student responsibility—allowing students to take leadership and ownership over the projects performed

5. Establishing community partnerships—allowing "students to learn about their communities, explore career possibilities, and work with diverse groups of individuals"

6. Planning ahead for service learning

7. Equipping students with knowledge and skills needed for service (Maryland State Department of Education, 2003)

When thoroughly and thoughtfully supported, service learning offers the potential of a profoundly transformative experience for students. At their best,

> service learning experiences put abstract classroom concepts into concrete form and increase students' content knowledge and higher order thinking skills, foster civic responsibility, and develop informed citizens who participate in their communities after graduation in personally and professionally relevant ways. Service learning facilitates an appreciation for the interconnectedness of individuals, the communities in which they live, and the resources required to sustain both. (Florida Gulf Coast University, 2015, para. 2)

For these effects to take place, it requires that service learning projects have the characteristics outlined in the seven standards described earlier. It can be a transformative experience for students and communities when they also reflect these qualities:

- usefulness to the community
- connection to the curriculum
- emphasis on student reflection
- consistent student ownership/leadership
- supportive community partnerships
- adult involvement to provide participation support for students
- comprehensive planning by teachers

The presence of these characteristics can make the difference between a feel-good project and a profoundly transformative experience. It can expand the potential range of career competencies for students and benefit the condition of communities and of U.S. civic life itself.

REFLECTION ACTIVITIES

Time for Reflection

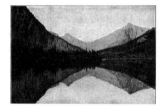

1. Consider Ted Sizer's (1984) characterization of the experience of high school students. How might the introduction of service learning projects address some of the harsher elements of that description?

2. Describe two or three problems that you can identify in your school or community and a type of community service project that could potentially offer opportunities for students to develop academic understanding and enhance skills and knowledge.

3. What current opportunities do students in your school have to develop citizenship skills and awareness? How could service learning extend such opportunities?

4. What are some potential challenges you see in instituting service learning in your setting?

Preparation for Service Learning Projects: A Protocol

As a rule, it is recommended that the following protocol or stages be implemented in service learning projects:

1. Investigation

2. Planning and preparation

3. Implementation

4. Reflection

5. Demonstration/celebration (RMC Research Corporation, 2009)

Let's look closely at each stage. As we do this, we will also look at some examples of how service learning helps to cultivate the educational partnerships that we've described throughout this book and the various spheres of influence that support student learning in a school community.

Investigation

During the first phase of service learning, students begin by assessing an area of need in their communities where their efforts could help solve or address a problem. This may be accomplished with discussion and brainstorming sessions. It also represents a powerful opportunity and context for student research. For example, some teachers have had students use clipboards and observational protocols to note what they find in their communities. They teach students how to use a type of "mapping" of conditions and problems that affect people's lives. Other teachers have provided students with newspapers and asked them to reflect systematically over a period of a week or two on the kinds of problems that reoccur in a community. Let's take a closer look at the type of mapping we are referring to.

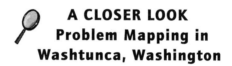

A CLOSER LOOK
Problem Mapping in
Washtunca, Washington

The U.S. Department of Agriculture funds and sponsors 4-H Clubs to offer training to young people in farming methods and practical life skills. It also offers training and technical assistance grants to groups in the community that want to help provide constructive activities to young people outside of school.

With the support of the National 4-H Council, a multiaged group of adults and youth in Washtunca, Washington, used a grant to facilitate a service learning project. Over a 2-year period, the group assessed the needs of the community, interviewed townspeople, held public meetings, and mapped the assets of the area. The mapping identified a lack of family- and youth-oriented activity as an area in which 4-H could make a difference. Young people benefited greatly. They learned how to participate in designing and offering the needed activities, including community dinners, classes, and clubs. There were also many intergenerational benefits. At the end of the project cycle, participants of various ages summarized what they had learned by working family to family throughout the service experience. The depth that participation offered is apparent in the following comments made by two high school students:

> "I learned more about my community, other communities, and how all communities are alike. Each town has problems; it doesn't matter how big or small it is."

"I learned how to write grants, how the government works, how different groups face different obstacles, and how to change the community for the better."

As one adult participant commented, "I learned to stand up for what I believe is best and right, regardless of what my best friend and a few others think." In addition to the practical skills taught and shared, it is clear that this kind of interaction encouraged perspective taking, which leads to understanding and the kind of social cohesion that makes communities (and young people) stronger and more resilient (Naughton, 2000).

The first phase includes surveying, fact finding, and brainstorming. Students then work in groups to make decisions about the focus of the project. They consider whether they want to address a problem that is global, national, regional, or simply schoolwide. Though the leadership of students is a powerful aspect of service learning, the learning needs of the class, as the teacher sees it, are important as well. The final choice for the focus of the project should be student led, with teachers providing guidance and input into the process and design. This allows students to take ownership, while giving teachers the flexibility to address what they see as the learning needs and priorities of the class.

As another important aspect of the investigation stage, students measure and record observations and data about the situation they are going to address. Using this information as a baseline, they look at the same conditions at the end of the project and are able to assess the effect that their work has had.

Planning and Preparation

Once the focus of the service learning activity is chosen, there are a number of vital planning and preparation decisions to be made collaboratively by students and teachers. These include choosing what the specific service offered by the class is going to be and determining what learning goals students will meet during the study. Teachers must also consider the practical training or background information that students will need in order to have the knowledge and skills to conduct the project. For example, they may need to know how to conduct interviews, how to use tools or scientific instruments, or simply learn more about the people or situations they are going to encounter.

In addition to the technical competencies, teachers may want to consider the citizenship and civic participation components of the curriculum that can be developed during the project that are much more effectively taught in a real-life context. Some examples include civics-related knowledge about how government and democracy functions, how to influence policy through advocacy, how to work on a common goal as a member of a team to advance the public good, and how to be an active and involved citizen. Let's look at two teachers, Louise Levy and Darryl Clark, from Belchertown, Massachusetts, as they engage in this stage.

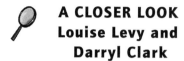

A CLOSER LOOK
Louise Levy and
Darryl Clark

Louise Levy, a science teacher at Belchertown High School, formed a partnership with Darryl Clark's second-grade classroom at Swift River Elementary School, which is located on the other side of a fence that separates the two schoolyards. After several years in which Louise's classes took part in the Harvard Forest Schoolyard Ecology program, Buds, Leaves and Global Warming, the town of Belchertown made two protected natural areas, Foley Field and Lake Wallace, available for use by the Belchertown Public Schools.

The teachers then began to bring their classes together to do schoolyard and recess explorations of native tree identification and fall leaf color change. In time, Darryl's class began to join the high school students in Levy's lab/classroom for flower dissection to learn the parts of the flower and to compare apple varieties as part of a lesson on how local ecosystems provide ecological services for human communities. They discussed the role of locally grown food in order to study changes in vernal pools. The second graders also took a field trip to the high school campus pond. Louise's students taught the second graders proper sampling methods and "respectful exploration" collecting, observing and counting with conscious care to do no harm to the pond organisms.

In each instance, the high school students were provided with support to enact the role of mentor and exploration partner with the younger students. The younger students were supported to learn partnering skills so that the excursions would have a lasting and meaningful influence on the collaborating students beyond the initial activity. The planning phase plays an important role in service learning. As in the case of these two teachers, planning well also lends itself to additional service learning activities for a wide variety of purposes. Louise describes the rationale for having older and younger students work and learn together, and she discusses how her partnership with Darryl expanded to include all of the elementary school's second-grade teachers.

With the success of this initial partnership came the Ecomentors (a K–12 program) and BEST Explorers (for girls in Grades 4–12). Such programs led to $15,000 in grants that gave the high school access to technology resources that might have otherwise been unaffordable to the district.

On the high school level, it's a lot harder to involve families, as teenagers tend to be drawing away to strike out on their own. Cross-grade partnerships are an idea to form relationships, though. They draw out the best in both sets of kids. You get a greater attention span. The little ones look up to the older ones and will learn more quickly, which will encourage my students to learn and internalize the material. The older students reconnect to the excitement they had when they were younger.

I designed Woodland/Honors Ecology to have as many hands-on activities as it possibly can. I have students who feel as if they haven't met with success and "invite them into the discourse community," building a sense of stewardship over the ecology and the sense of community.

We've been partnering with second grade, mostly through the persuasive power of my colleague Darryl Clark, so we can involve the entire second grade. For the last two Aprils, we have conducted field trips to Lake Wallace and had the second-grade teachers step outside the norm of how they run their classes. Some of the writing ideas, observation, math ideas that we used on the field trip were meant to be brought into the classroom, if the teachers wanted to take it one step further. Darryl had to sell the idea at first to his principal and colleagues, because it's really outside of what the practical emphasis is because of scheduling and the testing, but now colleagues in his school are becoming excited about it.

While her students led the service learning project, Louise worked closely with colleagues to ensure its capacity to be inclusionary by taking into account the various learning needs, learning styles, and diverse ages/grades of the students.

My students ran the whole thing, engaging teachers and chaperones so that it was similar to a museum field trip, building a foundation for a 4th-grade outdoor study trip. I engaged with the special education department to be able to support the high schoolers in this. We also involved parents, community members, and the school nurse. It took effort, but all of it led to a rich experience for the younger as well as the older students.

By including an entire grade, we have the opportunity to reach and engage students across differences in learning styles and success histories, and make it possible for all to have a feeling of inclusion and success. We support the conceptual understanding by preteaching a short list of vocabulary terms that have either a visual or active component to learning. The field trip activities allowed kids to get active, sampling the water with nets, sorting and counting—with no barriers with language or cognitive levels. We also made sure to include art and dance so there would be a component of multimodal learning. To bring in English language arts, the field trip includes an opportunity for high school students to do an assessment of their local knowledge in the form of a writing assignment titled "This Is Where I Live" in preparation for the New England Outdoor Writers Association's Youth Writing Contest, and we encourage students to submit their work to this.

For Louise, these service learning projects are not just extracurricular efforts, but practical ones that are essential to her success as a high school science teacher.

> If we don't provide younger students with engaging science, social studies, and project-based cooperative learning experiences from the start, we risk ending up with unmotivated high school science students who feel disenfranchised from the learning experience. If the interest wasn't there when they were younger, it becomes harder for them to care by the time we get them in high school, especially as classroom focus on intensive math and English language arts makes hands-on, experiential learning even more rare at the elementary level. We'd begun to see the leading edge of this trend showing among all our students who had grown up thinking that science was the study of reading passages followed by multiple-choice questions. Our motto this year is "to explore with joy, reverence, and relentless optimism." In truth, I can't stand in front of my students every day unless I explicitly let them know that I believe in every one of them.

Implementation

Leading up to the implementation stage has been information gathering and planning to guide and focus the effort. The actual implementation of the service learning project is where teachers offer the kinds of training experiences that prepare students and where students begin to offer their service. Teachers have a crucial role during implementation as they foster and encourage connections students may make between the service and the academic and civic skills that they may be learning through it. Implementation also involves ongoing critical reflection and problem solving by students and teachers as they consider the inevitable complications bound to emerge when their ideas meet real-life conditions. Service learning can also create opportunities for parents and guardians to stand in a different kind of relationship to schools, one in which they are seen as experts and are able to contribute meaningfully to the content of their children's education. This aspect highlights the spheres of influence that we have discussed throughout our book. As such, the partnerships between teachers and students, students and students, teachers and families, families and families, teachers and the school community, and the school community with the community at large become fully realized. Let's look at an elementary school example of this in practice as we continue to explore service learning.

A CLOSER LOOK
Forest Ranch
Elementary

At Forest Ranch Elementary School, in Forest Ranch, California, students and families helped create a school garden. This provided the school with healthy lunches and community food banks with surplus food. Cindy Triffo, a high school teacher and co-coordinator of service learning in the Chico Unified School District, said this project encouraged families at one school with a large population of Hmong and Hispanic families who work in the agricultural industry to get involved as horticultural experts, bringing them into a meaningful alliance with teachers and the school community.

In addition to this significant benefit, the garden project also gave high school students a focus for nutrition classes and a health fair focusing on gardening, cooking, and healthy eating and gave elementary students hands-on experience observing the life cycle and parts of plants. Local nurseries and excavation companies provided topsoil, and Habitat for Humanity and AmeriCorps volunteers helped students build garden beds. All the while students were involved in decision making, from elementary students deciding on what plants to grow to high school students planning and publicizing the health fair that had statewide outreach (Pearson Education, 2000–2014).

A CLOSER LOOK
Harvard Forest

Another rich example of service learning is the Harvard Forest Schoolyard Ecology project, which takes place across the United States on the grounds of schools and beyond. "We would become citizen scientists, participating in an important ecological study with distinguished scientists—on our school's own nature trail!" is how fifth-grade teacher Katherine Bennett (2010) of John R. Briggs Elementary School, in Ashburnham, Massachusetts, proudly described her students' work in collecting data and observations as part of a national network of sites involved in long term ecological research.

Harvard University maintains a 3,750-acre research forest in Petersham, Massachusetts. Among its programs is a collaboration with Bennett's students and many other K–12 teachers and students called the Schoolyard LTER (Long-Term Ecological Research) Program. There are 26 sites in this program around the country, and each one maintains partnerships with classrooms and schools. Participating teachers are trained and encouraged to involve their students in field-based research projects in which they directly observe and collect data on changes in forests, leaves, and vernal pools.

The idea of learning science in a genuine and useful social context is a powerful and motivating one to students. The teachers begin their involvement in the program by visiting the scientists at Harvard Forest and getting background and on-site training about how to make and record scientific observations. Students taking part in the study in their schoolyards become participants in a national data-gathering effort. With their clipboards and data sheets, they not only take on the role of scientists with the props and tools of the trade, but also learn to apply their (developing) skills in observation, measurement, and data recording (all integral parts of the English language arts and science frameworks as described by the Common Core State Standards [Common Core State Standards Initiative, 2014]) to a large-scale effort that is increasing the sum of human knowledge.

This program utilizes the power of relationships to give students a powerful context for learning curriculum. The idea of actual scientists reading and using the data that they collect gives meaning and purpose to their efforts. It also invites them into the professional community of scientists. As teachers are mentored by scientists, and students are mentored by teachers and sometimes directly by Harvard Forest scientists, the context of the activity changes from school performance to real-world participation.

By contributing to this study, students are transcending their role as students to be involved directly in the role of scientists following protocols, collecting data, making predictions, and thinking about what the data, collected over time, reveal and contribute to our understanding about patterns of ecological change that may be happening on a much larger level. Harvard Forest's educational coordinator, Pamela Snow, herself an experienced classroom teacher, explains:

> We have several goals for the program. At the heart of it is a sense of students connecting what they are doing to the real world to learn about science by having students entering into the role of scientists, which we hope makes acting as they do seem authentic, natural, and routine to them all at once.
>
> We're also interested in helping to give them a deeper connection with nature, by going out into it and learning to observe. It would be nice to think this work might result in young people eventually becoming working ecologists, but even where this doesn't happen, we are definitely "planting seeds." It could be that they go into ecology or become another kind of scientist, or it may simply be that they become informed citizens who know how to interpret data to support claims in making decisions. Both outcomes fulfill important aspects of our educational mission.

Reflection

Continuous reflection is a defining feature of effective service learning projects that makes it possible for students to identify and name their new understandings. It also enables them to solidify emerging and developing skills. Reflection may take a variety of forms, including, but not limited to, journals; reflective essays; in-class discussions; teacher prompts; role-plays; demonstrations; presentations to special audiences; poetic, musical, or dance projects; and more traditional academic papers.

Facilitating Reflection: A Manual for Leaders and Educators (Reed & Koliba, n.d.) features a collection of activities designed to give students and community partners different ways of integrating service learning experiences into new understanding using role-plays, discussions, and exercises. It offers an extensive list of options reflecting a belief that just as learners and learning styles are diverse, so should be the options available to educators in helping students draw conclusions and meaning from their experiences.

Demonstration/Celebration

The culminating events at the end of a service learning project help students integrate the discoveries and insights they developed throughout. These events also demonstrate to others beyond the classroom the effects of the project on the community and on the students themselves. The public recognition can help the participants feel a greater sense of appreciation for what was accomplished and reinforce students' dedication to public service. In the example below, a student project leads not only to an improvement in the community, but to support for the student's school itself.

> Students in an alternative school had been conducting water studies in the nearby watershed for years and received consistent recognition from the Bureau of Land Management for their efforts. The Bureau counted on these students to keep track of progress being made in reducing pollution. The students learned valuable skills in measuring various aspects of stream health. When the school district put the alternative school on the list for closure, due to budget cuts, the students and the Bureau partnered to develop a campaign for the school board to keep the school open. They went door to door to voters to tell them of the need for the school and the benefits for the community of having the school in place. Voters passed a tax levy and the board was convinced to keep the school open. (Billig, 2007)

Teachers have many choices for culminating events. The goal of these activities is to reinforce and extend the learning and the sense of efficacy students get from participating in service learning.

Student-created videos, PowerPoint presentations, poster and presentation showcases, and pre- and postmeasurements of understanding and skill can all serve as ways for students to demonstrate to others (and to themselves) just how much learning has occurred and how valuable a service learning project can be. Since service learning involves a learning community's shared sense of mission, it can be especially powerful to acknowledge and celebrate the conclusion of the group's work with a schoolwide assembly that recognizes the project's successes, a tour of the service site, letters of thanks from project recipients, as well as a presentation fair. Inviting and involving community partners in the celebration can also help to acknowledge and express gratitude and strengthen relationships for their future involvement.

Often the unanticipated insights that come from taking the perspectives of others are the most valuable and enduring results of a project, as in the following example from an Oklahoma City intergenerational service project.

REFLECTION ACTIVITIES

Time for Reflection

Reflect on the following questions and write a response.

1. What are some ways a teacher might tie in academic skills to the Investigation Stage even before the project is chosen?

2. How might students use the Reflection Stage to help them (and their teachers) document and demonstrate student use of high level thinking skills?

3. Explain why (or if) you believe that the Demonstration/Celebration phase is a mandatory part of any service learning project.

A CLOSER LOOK
Make a
Difference Day

Last year the program integrated senior citizens into their youth activities by cohosting an internet workshop for elders on Make a Difference Day in October. Several organizations joined in the event at Oklahoma City Community College, where youth and students used their Vietnamese language skills to set up email accounts for the seniors and show them how to "surf the net" for sites related to health, Vietnamese culture, cooking, and medical information. "When we had the internet workshop we could see three generations right there—the parents, the grandparents, and the youth. We had three generations sitting down at one computer," says [Community Coordinator Dong] Bui. "The youth learned that working with the elderly is fun. Before they thought the elderly were so old, that they don't want to know about anything, that they don't understand the youth. And then after working with them they are laughing together and the elderly invited them to lunch."

Kim Doan, 15, said participating in the internet workshop helped her see the value of some of her classes in school. "I learned all about computers in school, so then at the workshop I could help the elderly learn about it, too," she says. "That's just one example of how I use what I learn to help in service projects" (Naughton, 2000).

REFLECTION ACTIVITIES

Time for Reflection

Reflect on the following questions and write a response.

1. What are some academic, personal, and civic skills that students can attain through service learning that are much harder to teach in traditional classroom work? Give four to seven examples.

2. Why do you think so much of the literature on service learning places such strong emphasis on the need for students to engage in ongoing reflection at all stages of the project?

3. In considering each of the five stages of planning and conducting a service learning project described in this chapter, what are some ways that a teacher can give a gradual release of responsibility and ownership to students?

4. Consider a potential service learning project that addresses a need in the school community you know best. How might you use this project to help activate and extend partnerships within the six spheres of influence (teacher/student, student/student, teacher/family, family/family, teacher/school community, and school community/community at large) that we consider in this book?

Summary

In this chapter we looked at service learning as an important partnership practice. We described its historic roots as well as contemporary issues of equal access to it. Further, we showed how it is a critical means of providing an authentic real-world context for social interaction between students, peers, teachers, and the larger community. We also discussed how it enhances students' academic and civic knowledge and skills. We described five stages of a service learning project and provided many examples in practice. We also considered how the benefits of service learning include increased motivation and engagement for students as well as greater involvement of families and community partners in the success of all learners.

In our final chapter, we will discuss how this book can be used for professional growth purposes.

References

Bennett, K. (2010). Citizen scientists. *Science and Children, 48*(1), 50–55. Retrieved from http://harvardforest.fas.harvard.edu/sites/harvardforest.fas.harvard.edu/files/publications/pdfs/Bennett_Science&Children_2010.pdf

Billig, S. (2007). *Unpacking what works in service learning.* Retrieved from http://www.nylc.org/sites/nylc.org/files/files/323unpacking.pdf

Center for Civic Education. (1994). *National standards for civics and government.* Calabasas, CA: Author.

Common Core State Standards Initiative. (2014). *English language arts standards: Science and technical subjects: Grade 6–8: 3.* Retrieved from http://www.corestandards.org/ELA-Literacy/RST/6-8/3

Education Commission of the States. (2014). *Service learning: Quick facts.* Retrieved from http://www.ecs.org/html/IssueSection.asp?issueid=109&s=Quick+Facts

Florida Gulf Coast University. (2015). *Service learning.* Retrieved from http://www.fgcu.edu/Connect/index.html

Giles, D. E., & Eyler, J. (1994). The theoretical roots of service learning in John Dewey: Toward a theory of service learning. *Michigan Journal of Community Service Learning, 1*(1), 74–85.

Grant, A. M. (2008). The significance of task significance: Job performance effects, relational mechanisms, and boundary conditions. *Journal of Applied Psychology, 93*(1), 108–124.

Grant, A. M., & Parker, S. K. (2009). Redesigning work design theories: The rise of relational and proactive perspectives. *Academy of Management Annals, 3,* 317–375.

Guilfoyle, L., & Ryan, M. (2013). *Linking service-learning and the Common Core State Standards: Alignment, progress, and obstacles.* Denver, CO: Education Commission of the States.

KIDS Consortium. (2011). *Playground shade.* Retrieved from http://www.kidsconsortium.org/playground_shade.php

Los Angeles Unified School District. (n.d.). *Service learning lesson plans.* Retrieved from http://notebook.lausd.net/portal/page?_pageid=33,179449&_dad=ptl

Maryland State Department of Education. (2003). *Maryland's 7 best practices of service-learning.* Retrieved from http://www.marylandpublicschools.org/MSDE/programs/servicelearning/7_best_practices.htm

National Youth Leadership Council. (n.d.-a). *Activating education excellence through service-learning.* Retrieved from http://www.nylc.org/sites/nylc.org/files/GCS%20Statistics%20Graphs.pdf

National Youth Leadership Council. (n.d.-b). *What is service learning?* Retrieved from http://nylc.advantagelabs.com/sites/nylc.org/files/wisl/index.html

Naughton, S. (2000). *Youth and communities helping each other: Community-based organizations using service learning as a strategy during out-of-school time.* Washington, DC: Corporation for National Service. Retrieved from https://www.nationalserviceresources.gov/files/r1803-youth-and-communities-helping-each-other.pdf

Pearson Education. (2000–2014). *Service-learning case study: Chico, CA.* Retrieved from https://www.teachervision.com/volunteer-work/resource/4965.html?page=1

Reed, J., & Koliba, C. (n.d.). *Facilitating reflection: A manual for leaders and educators.* Retrieved from http://www.uvm.edu/~dewey/reflection_manual

RMC Research Corporation. (2009). *K–12 service-learning project-planning toolkit.* Scotts Valley, CA: National Service-Learning Clearinghouse. Retrieved from http://www.ode.state.or.us/teachlearn/specialty/servicelearning/k-12-service-learning-project-planning-toolkit.pdf

Ryan, M. (2012). *Service learning after Learn and Serve America: How five states are moving forward.* Denver, CO: Education Commission of the States. Retrieved from http://www.ecs.org/clearinghouse/01/02/87/10287.pdf

Sizer, T. R. (1984). *Horace's compromise: The dilemma of the American high school.* Boston: Houghton Mifflin Harcourt.

Spring, K., & Grimm, R. (2008). *Community service and service learning in America's schools.* Washington, DC: Corporation for National and Community Service, Office of Research and Policy Development.

Turner, Y. N., Hadas-Halperin, I., & Raveh, D. (2008, November). *Patient photos spur radiologist empathy and eye for detail.* Paper presented at the annual meeting of the Radiological Society of North America.

8

Using Learning Partnerships in Professional Development

Applying the Ideas

Be the change you want to see in the world.

—Gandhi

> What kinds of professional growth activities will help us build partnerships for the purpose of advancing equity, engagement, and achievement among our dynamically changing student populations?

Donna Hendricks, a sixth-grade social studies and English language arts teacher in Ohio, serves on the professional development team at her school. As in many of our schools, her school's student population represents diverse socioeconomic, racial, ethnic, cultural, and language groups as well as a sweeping range of academic and literacy skills. Her school community has been intentional about including its students' various cultures and histories in its curriculum. Donna makes it a point to include these concepts and resources in her lessons, as she wants all of her students and their families to be active contributors in her classroom community. She is also familiar with concepts about low- and high-status students (Banks, 2008; Cohen, 1994; Cohen & Lotan, 2014; Zacarian, 2013) and the influence that this has on their outcomes. She has just finished reading our book and is beginning to form some ideas for enacting professional development activities that she would like included. She wants professional development to be useful and transformative for her colleagues and to strengthen everyone's practice.

All of us have been part of teacher preparation programs, and those of us in the field have engaged in professional development as part of our continued education and/or district's requirements. We would likely say that some of these learning experiences were great and others were ineffective or even discouraging. Further, some of us might admit that we are oversaturated with things that we have collected in professional development that we somehow cannot dispose of but are not really being used or haven't been the best at getting the needed results. If we were to go through our storage area of tools to figure out what to save and use and what to throw out, how many tools made a lasting impression and helped us transform our thinking and our practice? The key to education, like professional development, is in being able to integrate information by making it ours. It is not about taking on new manufactured procedures and ideas; it is about the slow work of manufacturing our own understanding through social interaction, through our own thinking and sifting and encountering new information thoughtfully and in context.

Drawing on our experiences, what kinds of things would we suggest that Donna think about to best ensure that the professional development experience is positive and long-lasting?

REFLECTION ACTIVITIES

Time for Reflection

Reflect on the following questions and write a response.

1. What types of learning activities do you believe are essential for your preferred style of learning as you address your professional growth? Describe two or three activities that you would want to take part in.

2. What conditions do you believe are critical for sustained and ongoing professional development?

What Is Critical for Professional Growth?

Key to learning, including what we do to professionally strengthen our work, is being able to integrate new information by making it our own. It is not about taking on new manufactured procedures and ideas; it is about the slow work of manufacturing our own understanding through social interaction, through our own thinking, and by encountering and sifting through new information thoughtfully and in context. Perhaps one of the largest complexities facing us today is the rapidly increasing volume of diversity in student and family populations against the backdrop of a professional community that is predominantly white, monolingual English speaking, and middle class (Ahmad & Boser, 2014; Dilworth & Coleman, 2014; Hollins & Guzman, 2005; Medina, Morrone, & Anderson, 2005). While we want our students to do well in school and be active, thoughtful, and responsive members of their learning communities and beyond, we know that we must understand and use practices that are effective with our dynamically changing population of students and their families. Here is an example of this complexity in practice as it relates to the Common Core State Standards (CCSS) for sixth-grade mathematics. It calls for students to "use ratio and rate reasoning to solve real-world and mathematical problems, e.g., by reasoning about tables of equivalent ratios, tape diagrams, double number line diagrams, or equations" (Common Core State Standards Initiative, 2014). Here is a math problem furnished by the CCSS:

CCSS.MATH.CONTENT.6.RP.A.3.B

For example, if it took 7 hours to mow 4 lawns, then at that rate, how many lawns could be mowed in 35 hours? At what rate were lawns being mowed? (Common Core State Standards Initiative, 2014)

Most of us reading this example can picture a lawn being mowed. Some of us mow our own lawns, have earned money mowing other people's lawns, or maybe grew up being the designated family lawn mower. As such, we have depth of knowledge in this type of activity and can easily "see" the math problem presented. Conversely, many students have no experience seeing, walking on, or being near a lawn, let alone mowing it. This includes the large number of students who live in urban areas where lawns are nonexistent. Another case in point is Barbara Rothenberg, a second-grade teacher from Amherst, Massachusetts, who invited her students and their families to her home to pick apples. While many participated in the social event, several of her guests had no knowledge that apples grew on trees and/or in Amherst. They came to her home believing that they would be going on a field trip to the local supermarket to "get" apples. These examples show us how much we can take for granted and miss. To develop professionally requires us to develop a heightened awareness of our students and their families so that we can be more certain that our learning communities are accessible and engaging. Professional development spaces are natural settings for this to occur as they offer all of us the opportunity to explore new ideas, deliberate on them, and transform our practices.

The professional learning association Learning Forward (2014) defines professional development as "a comprehensive, sustained, and intensive approach to improving teachers' and principals' effectiveness in raising student achievement." This definition is helpful for individuals who wish to engage in self-study as a means for professional growth. In this book, we provide reflection spaces for two types of professional growth: individual self-study as well as group self-study for teachers such as Donna Hendricks, professional developers, and teacher educators who are involved in the planning and implementation of professional development as part of their school or district plan or for institutions of higher education that are preparing educators. While the book may be used for self-study, our hope is that in reading it you are supported in your belief that partnership learning is a powerful tool not just for students but for professionals as well—and that nothing is so persuasive to students as when we practice what we preach with our students, their families, the school community, and the community at large through engaging in book study partnerships. To push our point, we hope that in reading this chapter, you will be more empowered to use a method that we use with our students: learning together!

Throughout the book, we continuously use the word *partnerships* to describe the type of reciprocal relationships that we believe are necessary in the enterprise that we all know as public education. As such, we believe that partnerships are key dimensions for professional growth. We believe that professional development, in institutions of higher education and public and public charter school settings, should be partnership efforts that are

- inclusive of all students and their families,
- a collective responsibility,
- a well-prepared opportunity for professional growth,
- a consistent and routinized event that occurs on a regular basis,
- an opportunity for teams to analyze and reflect on student work and what it says about the thinking of the young people who created it to try to make ever more thoughtful and effective teaching decisions.

Why Is Book Study an Important Format?

Book study gives us the opportunity to collectively explore and examine a common set of ideas by thinking about and interacting with them. Whether it is planned and delivered by a teacher educator in a higher education institution, an expert coming in to a district, educators attending a conference to listen to an expert, or a group of colleagues gathering as a professional learning community, its intent is to examine ideas and come to collective agreement about how these might be employed in the real world of public education. One type might be called an *all-knowing authority perspective* in which there is one expert who has some important information to share to a passive listener. Another might be called *two all-knowing authority perspectives* in which the interactions between two parties move from one all-knowing authority to another, with neither changing his or her thinking or practice. Further, this type of conversation may occur in pairs or with others listening passively. A transformative interactive process is one that we might describe as *participants constructing common language, knowledge, and ways of thinking and acting through valuing and honoring each other's perspectives* (Zacarian, 2013). These three types are referred to as *my-o-logue, di-o-logue,* and *our-o-logue* (Zacarian, 2013). We believe that an our-o-logue is essential for us to be open to each other's perspectives and be willing to adopt and share effective ideas, whether they are our own or those of our colleagues, to support the growth of students.

Structure for Professional Book Study

Book study, whether by individuals or groups, should occur on an established schedule over a sustained period of time such as a semester or school term or a designated number of periodic sessions. This provides time to read the material, engage in the reflection activities found in the body of each chapter, and, in the case of those of us who are currently teaching, integrate the ideas meaningfully into our practice.

Collaborative Book Study

For those of us who wish to use a collaborative book study format, including college professors or professional development specialists, such as Donna Hendricks, plans for extended collaborative study and infusion of the ideas and practices is essential. In this case, there should be plans for separating participants into small groups with enough time allocated for each member to read assigned chapters and explore the ideas that are used through authentic tasks or activities in addition to the ones that may be furnished in the body of each chapter. For example, it is ideal for participants to visit actual school classrooms and family events or reflect on their own practices for a prescribed assignment or task so that the ideas that are provided in the book may be explored in context. There should also be consideration given to assigning key roles and activities for a collaborative book study format.

Obviously, at the very least, a book study group requires at least two participants. In the case of a college classroom, school, or district, it is ideal when participants are separated into groups of four to allow for paired and groupwork throughout the study process. Drawing from Cohen (1994), Cohen and Lotan (2014), Zacarian (2013), and Zacarian and Haynes (2012), each group should include some assigned roles to ensure that the group's process is as smooth as possible. We suggest that the roles include a facilitator to help prepare for meetings as well as a timekeeper during the meeting. Our rationale for the facilitator is threefold. First, the role helps to provide structure for the group meetings. Second, it is intended to guide the group in its interactive process. Third, it is intended to keep the group's work moving forward. The facilitator role may be a rotating one or enacted by the same person. It is important to note that the facilitator is not the authority of the group; rather, it is a member of the group. And the timekeeper's role is to ensure that the group remains on schedule. In addition to these two roles, we recommend that observational protocols, interviews, and self-reflection activities be included to support an authentic examination of what is being studied.

Drawing from Zacarian and Haynes (2012, p. 114), here are the facilitator's tasks:

Pre-Meeting Activities

- Identifying chapter focus questions and observational tasks
- Scheduling a kick-off "organizational" meeting to discuss the book group structure and calendar for group meetings as well as determining the length and schedule for each book study meeting
- Ensuring that the group knows the chapter, chapter focus questions, and chapter observational task assignments and date these are due

During-Meeting Activities

- Helping the group to stay focused on its collective task by guiding the group forward and keeping its collective discussion flowing
- Ensuring that each member has a voice and that every participant listens to others
- Assigning a timekeeper to ensure that the meeting flows smoothly

Conclusion/Meeting Wrap-Up Activities

- Creating a group review of its group process (e.g., what went well and what needs strengthening)
- Creating a review of group product (e.g., what was learned by observing and reading the chapter and how this will be applied to actual work and assessed for its effectiveness)

We devote this final chapter to this type of book study format with this book. Our intent is that participants can explore the ideas through four different venues: book study interactions and accompanying interview, survey, observation, and reflection tasks and activities. Figure 8.1 provides a recommended guide for book study activities. As in Zacarian and Haynes (2012), we allocate 90 minutes per book study meeting. The timing can be adjusted up or down, as deemed appropriate to your particular context. We want this to be a meaningful, practical, and informative process for all participants.

Figure 8.1   Book Study Format

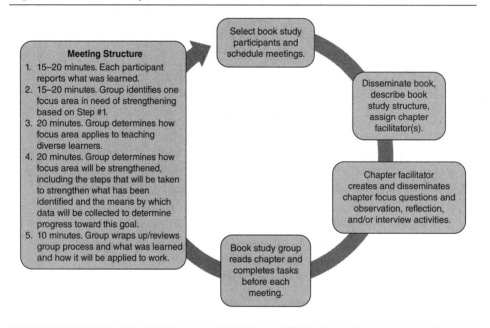

Source: Adapted from Zacarian & Haynes (2012, p. 115).

Interview Tasks and Activities

Interviews are a helpful means for understanding student, family, teacher, school community, and community-at-large populations. They enable us to form questions and gather information that we might not otherwise consider, understand perspectives other than our own, and deepen our individual and collective thinking about the populations that make up the whole of what we know as school.

Survey Tasks and Activities

Much of the data that we collect about our students may be centered on their performance on high-stakes tests and rate of absenteeism. The two are often used to seek new ways for making improvements. However, using this data may be challenging for a number of reasons. First, while state education departments and our own districts may disaggregate the results into subgroup categories, it is generally done in a wide swath. For example, let's say that most Latino students in a specific school district perform successfully on the state tests that they are given. Before we congratulate them and ourselves, are we sure that we have analyzed the data deeply or drilled down enough to know whether this is *all* Latino students or a subset that may or may not be representative of the larger population? The same holds true for absenteeism. While we might see that certain groups of students (e.g., students receiving free or reduced lunch) are absent from school, what kinds of data are we collecting on this challenge to disaggregate the data (drill down) more deeply to identify the root causes and remedies? The activities that we provide in this chapter are intended to be more purposeful about how to identify and address trends that are occurring as they occur so that our partnership efforts are purposeful and meaningful.

Observation Tasks and Activities

Observational protocols have been identified as a helpful means for understanding the practice of teaching as well as what is working and what needs strengthening (Calderón & Minaya-Rowe, 2011; Echevarria, Vogt, & Short, 2008; Zacarian, 2013). We have used these extensively to help support our professional practice and, specifically, the interactive spaces that we advocate in our book. As with the survey tasks and activities, the observation tasks and activities found in this chapter are intended to strengthen your understanding of students and families and, in turn, the academic success of students as well as their membership in and contributions to school communities and beyond.

Reflection Activities

Solo and collaborative reflection activities greatly help us understand what we are learning in connection with our prior experiences as well as our collective understanding about working with diverse populations. To do this effectively means that we are willing to think deeply and consider various points of view and perspectives about our personal and professional beliefs. We identify two types of reflection: what we do on the spot to make a moment-to-moment decision and how we reflect back to what we did or experienced (Schön, 1987). Both are critical for partnership learning (Wade, Fauske, & Thompson, 2008).

Each of the previous chapters includes related tasks and activities. In this chapter, we add interview, survey, observation, and/or reflection activities for each chapter. We encourage you to engage in all or some these tasks and activities and to create your own. Our goal is that we expand our thinking and practice so that our students are more successful as learners and actively involved members of their classroom, school, community, and beyond.

Book Study Activities

ACTIVITIES FOR CHAPTER 1:
What It Means to Be "In It Together" in Education

Focus Questions to Be Examined

- What changes have occurred in student populations?
- What is the difference between partnership and relationship building?

Survey Tasks and Activities

Each school, district, and state collects data about its student populations by subgroup and graduate rates. These can generally be found by doing a search of the website of a school or district, state department of education, or the U.S. Department of Education. For example, if we wanted to know about California's graduation rates, we can go to the U.S. Department of Education website (http://eddataexpress.ed.gov/data-element-explorer.cfm/tab/data/deid/127), where we see the information on graduation rates depicted in Figure 8.2.

Figure 8.2   California 2011–2012 Graduation Rates

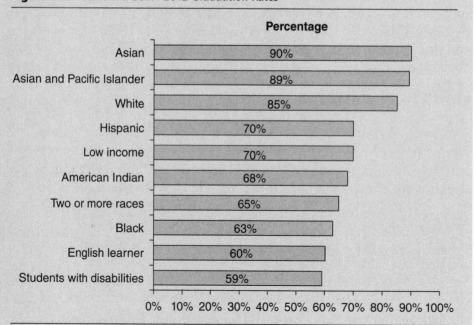

Source: U.S. Department of Education (2014).

1. Examine the changes that have occurred in student populations in your school, district, or state by taking a survey of 5 years of the following data.

Changes in student population year to year	Year 1	Year 2	Year 3	Year 4	Year 5
Total student population					
White					
Free or reduced lunch (i.e., low income)					
Hispanic/Latino					
Black					
Students with disabilities					
English learners					
Asian and Pacific Islander					
American Indian/Alaskan Native					

2. Examine the changes that have occurred in graduation rates in your school, district, or state by reviewing 3–5 years of graduation data. (Note: If this is not available to you, look at the most recent year of graduation data.)

Percentage graduating	Year 1	Year 2	Year 3	Year 4	Year 5
Total student population					
White					
Free or reduced lunch (i.e., low income)					
Hispanic/Latino					
Black					
Students with disabilities					
English learners					
Asian and Pacific Islander					
American Indian/Alaskan Native					

Reflection Activities

Respond to the following questions:

1. Based on the 5 years of data that you collected about student populations, what specific changes, if any, have occurred in the school, district, or state that you examined?

(Continued)

(Continued)

2. Based on the data that you collected on graduation rates, what changes, if any, have occurred in the school, district, or state that you examined?

3. Chapter 1 highlights the need for various partnerships: teacher-student; student-student; teacher-parent; parent-parent; teacher–school community; and school community–community at large. Discuss the changes that you have found in student demographics and outcomes and the reasons why partnerships are an important consideration.

ACTIVITIES FOR CHAPTER 2:
An Involved Classroom Community

Focus Questions to Be Examined

- What one or two sentences from the chapter resonated the most with you?
- How did the chapter inform your beliefs about partnerships and student engagement?
- How did the chapter inform your knowledge of different beliefs about partnerships?
- How did the chapter inform your beliefs about the spheres of influence on relationships, student engagement, and family involvement?

Observation Tasks and Activities

1. Observe a lesson from start to finish, and complete the following tasks during the observation. This may occur in a public school, college, or other educational setting. The purpose is to note the amount of student interaction that occurs.

   Note the start time of the lesson. _____

   Note the end time of the lesson. _____

   How much time elapses between when the lesson begins and when students interact?

   What is the dominant format of the class?

   ☐ Teacher-led

   ☐ Students working in pairs

   ☐ Students working in groups

   ☐ A combination of teacher-led and students in pairs

☐ A combination of teacher-led and students in groups
☐ Other (describe)

Does every student interact at the same rate throughout the lesson? What differences do you note among different students?

2. If possible, observe a parent conference/interaction.

Note the start time of the meeting. _____

Note the end time of the meeting. _____

How much time elapses between when the meeting begins and when a parent actively interacts?

How many total minutes consisted of school personnel speaking? _____

How many total minutes consisted of families or their representatives speaking? _____

What is the dominant format of the meeting?
☐ Teacher-led
☐ An even combination of teacher-parent interaction
☐ Other (describe)

ACTIVITIES FOR CHAPTER 3:
Infusing the Assets of Students and Families Into Classroom Learning

Focus Questions to Be Examined

- What are some ways that teacher language and actions can unintentionally create barriers to participation for families?
- What are some steps educators can take to facilitate greater family participation in children's learning lives in and out of school?
- What might be the primary goals of family participation in classroom activity? What constitutes "meaningful" family participation?

(Continued)

(Continued)

Observation Tasks and Activities

1. Create a collection of examples of communication that is intended to support families to be aware and active in what their children are learning and doing in school. Include such items as these:

   o classroom newsletters
   o schoolwide notes
   o class websites
   o school handbooks
   o PowerPoints or scripts for curriculum nights
   o videos of you or colleagues addressing families on curriculum nights or other special occasions

2. Locate and quote specific examples of where the wording acknowledges or takes into account the diverse circumstances of your students' families in regard to the following:

   o nontraditional family structure
   o language and culture diversity
   o differences in economic resources
   o gender-neutral language
   o level of linguistic sophistication

3. Assess the formality/informality of the tone of language found in activity #2. Find examples to support your assessment. Look for and record examples of where any of the descriptors below apply:

   o caring
   o respect for diversity
   o excessive formality
   o inclusiveness
   o intimidating
   o emotional safety
   o friendly

Reflection Activities

Respond to the following questions:

1. What are some examples of language in these communications that seem effective at communicating respect for families and inviting their further involvement?

2. How would you change these communications to make them more inclusive of the differences among families, particularly those who may need support to get more involved in a partnership with their children's school?

3. What strategies, messages, and phrasing do you think are important to employ when communicating with families who have limited use of English, are in single-parent households, face financial hardship, have limited formal education, or are nontraditional families?

ACTIVITIES FOR CHAPTER 4:
Preparing for Classroom Community

Focus Questions to Be Examined

- Students in a new classroom can be like an iceberg, with only a small percentage of their totality visible "above the water." What essential information about students would you like to be familiar with as the school year begins?
- What are some things that you would be interested in and willing to try to be as aware as possible of the personal history and current factors that have influenced your students as people and as learners?
- What are some ways you can create trust and communicate a sense of deep regard and respect at the outset of your work with students and families that will serve everyone well in the school year ahead as the year begins?
- How can you help to de-escalate the anxiety of the unknown experienced by everyone at the start of a new school year as a group of strangers begins ambitious work together?

Survey Tasks and Activities

People in any profession can be resistant to change, and for good reason. Once there is stability in established practice, a kind of invisible force field holds it in place, as the professional community tends to regard new ideas as destabilizing and pushes back on them with doubts and challenges.

Consider the force field that exists around changing customary, traditional teacher-student and teacher-family relationships. With your group, develop a consensus description of how teachers at your school come to know families and students versus ways that are described in this chapter (assuming they are different).

(Continued)

(Continued)

As a group, create a Pro and Con T-chart that first gives reasons for why the customary practices serve well and do not need to be changed (Pro), then lists reasons that other practices such as those described in this chapter are needed (Con).

1. Have group members rank each statement on a scale of 1–5 fingers, with 5 meaning *strongly agree*, 4 meaning *agree*, 3 meaning *neutral*, 2 meaning *disagree*, and 1 meaning *strongly disagree*. Give each person time to explain her or his rankings without comment from the other group members.

2. Allow each group member time to comment or reflect on how his or her attitudes were affected by the discussion and how these attitudes may have changed or strengthened as a result of the points raised.

Reflection Activities

After reading, have group members choose one to three quotes from the chapter that they agreed with, disagreed with, or that encouraged them to think about their practice in a new way. Give each participant up to 3 minutes to read a quote(s) and describe why she or he selected it. Invite the other members of the group to respond to the quote(s) using these prompts:

1. What is your response to what you just heard? Does this match your experience? Do you see things differently?

2. What are the implications of this idea for your own practice? How might you change what you do next year in light of what you are coming to understand about how to begin a school year in a way that supports the best outcomes for your students?

ACTIVITIES FOR CHAPTER 5:
The Academic Learning Benefits of Being "In It Together"

Focus Questions to Be Examined

- What aspects of the emotional climate of a classroom can positively affect learning?
- In what ways do diversity and differences among students represent an advantage to the learning environment? What are some challenges that teachers need to take into account to help students be successful in a classroom populated by students of diverse abilities, home experiences, and cultural and linguistic backgrounds?

Interview Tasks and Activities

1. Observe a classroom where group activities, such as cooperative learning, are occurring. Note groups where students appear engaged and easily cooperative as well as challenged by the tasks and delayed in their apparent progress.

2. Select a pair or group of students that appeared to be at ease and productive in their groupwork as well as one that seemed to be encountering difficulties in their tasks. Record their answer to questions such as these:

   o What work has your class done that helped you know how to be successful when working with partners?
   o Do you feel your ideas were respected by your partner in the work you just did? How do you know?
   o When someone in your group has a hard time staying on task, how do you help them?
   o Did you feel safe to make a mistake or try out an idea you were unsure of? What did your partner(s) do to help create this atmosphere?
   o What is something that your teacher did that helped your class feel like a place where all students were accepted?
   o What is something that another student has done or said that made you trust that you could work with them?
   o What is your role in making your class feel like a safe place to learn and share ideas?
   o How did it feel to be doing this work together? What words or actions by your partners and teachers helped create this impression?

3. Talk with the classroom teacher as well. Ask questions such as these.

   o What work has your class done that helped you and them know how to be successful when working with partners?
   o What do you do to help students feel safe to make a mistake or try out ideas they are unsure of?
   o What is something a student has done or said to make you feel that they are collaborative with the process and task of groupwork?
   o What responsibilities do you assign to students in helping to make the class feel like a safe place to learn and share ideas?
   o How would you assess the level of student cooperation during this lesson? What words or actions by students helped create this impression?

4. Write a summary of important insights you gained from student and teacher responses to these questions. Be ready to share them with your group and get their responses.

ACTIVITIES FOR CHAPTER 6:
Using Classroom Events to Empower Students and Families

Focus Questions to Be Examined

- How do classroom events empower students and families?
- What are some of the key components of planning and enacting classroom events?
- What are some of the key barriers to participation?

Interview Tasks and Activities

1. Interview a classroom teacher about all of the family events that he or she holds throughout a school year. Inquire and take detailed notes about the types of events using the following list.

   o community-building events for social purposes
   o showcasing curriculum for making learning transparent
   o drawing on the rich resources of families
   o building home/school shared culture of learning

2. Interview a second classroom teacher about all of the family events that he or she holds throughout a school year. Inquire and take detailed notes about the types of events using the list described in #1.

Suggested Survey Activities

1. Have each member of a learning community complete a survey about all of the family events that she or he holds within a specific period of time (e.g., a semester) using the categories in the following table. Using the table, have each member note the categories and frequency of activities that occur.

Event type	Community-building events for social purposes	Showcasing curriculum for making learning transparent	Drawing on the rich resources of families	Building home/school shared culture of learning

2. Ask each member to keep a roster of participating families and any trends that she or he notes in terms of who attends which events and who does not. The trends might include mothers versus fathers, families of fluent English speakers versus families of English learners, families of children receiving free or reduced lunch, or any category that is helpful for collecting data for strengthening classroom events and family involvement in them.

Reflection Tasks and Activities

Based on the interview and suggested survey activities:

- What trends do you note about the types of activities that occurred?
- What changes would you suggest to broaden the type of events and strengthen classroom events?

ACTIVITIES FOR CHAPTER 7:
Widening the Circle Beyond the
Classroom: Service Learning

Focus Questions to Be Examined

- Why is service learning an essential component in a child's education?
- What are some key service learning disparities, and what is the rationale for these disparities?
- What are some of the key elements for successful service learning experiences?
- What protocol should be used to prepare for service learning projects?

Reflection Activities

Design a service learning activity based on a curriculum standard that is being taught or might be taught in the future.

1. Draw from the seven essential elements of successful service learning programs to describe how the project does the following:

   o meets a recognized need in the community
   o achieves curricular objectives through service learning—allowing classroom knowledge to be applied and tested in real-life settings
   o engages in reflection activities in the form of discussions, journaling, performing, writing, etc.
   o develops student responsibility—allowing students to take leadership and ownership over the projects performed
   o establishes community partnerships—allowing "students to learn about their communities, explore career possibilities, and work with diverse groups of individuals"
   o plans ahead for service learning
   o equips students with knowledge and skills needed for service (Maryland State Department of Education, 2003)

(Continued)

(Continued)

2. Drawing from the protocol for service learning, describe the following for your service learning project:

   o investigation
   o planning and preparation
   o implementation
   o reflection
   o demonstration/celebration

ACTIVITIES FOR CHAPTER 8:
Using Learning Partnerships in Professional
Development: Applying the Ideas

Focus Questions to Be Examined

- What is critical for professional development?
- Why is book study an important format?
- What pre-meeting, during-meeting, and wrap-up activities should be included?

Interview, Survey, Observation, and Reflection Tasks and Activities

In this book, we have provided examples and a model for participants and providers of professional development. We also want to encourage a meaningful and collaborative experience for you and colleagues as you work with the book's ideas. We want to extend an invitation to use this book and professional development chapter to deepen your collective practice. Our hope is that you will feel encouraged to put into practice what we want for our students:

- for all members of your learning community to be seen as sources of expertise and knowledge
- for learning to be an invitation
- for diverse perspectives to be seen as an asset
- for learners to be involved as active participants in framing questions and choosing tasks

To this end, we hope that you will write study questions and design activities for the unique needs and insights of participants in your particular context so that all will feel a sense of being "in it together" on behalf of the students of your schools, your communities, and your ever more interdependent world.

References

Ahmad, F. Z., & Boser, U. (2014). *America's leaky pipeline for teachers of color: Getting more teachers of color into the classroom.* Washington, DC: Center for American Progress. Retrieved from https://www.americanprogress.org/issues/race/report/2014/05/04/88960/americas-leaky-pipeline-for-teachers-of-color

Banks, J. (April 2008). Diversity, group identity, and citizenship education in the digital age. *Educational Researcher, 37*(3), 129–139.

Calderón, M. E., & Minaya-Rowe, L. (2011). *Preventing long-term ELs: Transforming schools to meet core standards.* Thousand Oaks, CA: Corwin.

Cohen, E. G. (1994). *Designing groupwork: Strategies for the heterogeneous classroom* (2nd ed.). New York, NY: Teachers College Press.

Cohen, E. G., & Lotan, R. (2014). *Designing groupwork: Strategies for the heterogeneous classroom* (10th ed.). New York, NY: Teachers College Press.

Common Core State Standards Initiative. (2014). *Grade 6: Ratios and proportional relationships.* Retrieved from http://www.corestandards.org/Math/Content/6/RP

Dilworth, M. E., & Coleman, M. J. (2014). *Time for a change: Diversity in teaching revisited.* Washington, DC: National Education Association. Retrieved from http://www.nea.org/assets/docs/Time_for_a_Change_Diversity_in_Teaching_Revisited_(web).pdf

Echevarria, J., Vogt, M. E., & Short, D. J. (2008). *Making content comprehensible for English learners: The SIOP model* (3rd ed.). Boston, MA: Allyn & Bacon.

Hollins, E., & Guzman, M. T. (2005). Research on preparing teachers for diverse populations. In M. Cochran Smith & K. M. Zeichner (Eds.), *Studying teacher education: The report of the AERA panel on research and teacher education* (pp. 477–548). Mahwah, NJ: Lawrence Erlbaum.

Learning Forward. (2014). *System leaders.* Retrieved from http://learningforward.org/system-leaders#.VHX-UovF8iq

Maryland State Department of Education. (2003). *Maryland's 7 best practices of service-learning.* Retrieved from http://www.marylandpublicschools.org/MSDE/programs/servicelearning/7_best_practices.htm

Medina, M. A., Morrone, S. A., & Anderson, J. A. (2005, May–June). The relevance of educational psychology to teacher education. *The Clearing House,* pp. 207–212.

Schön, D. A. (1987). *Educating the reflective practitioner.* San Francisco, CA: Jossey-Bass.

U.S. Department of Education. (2014). *Regulatory adjusted cohort graduation rate, all students: 2010–11.* Retrieved from http://eddataexpress.ed.gov/data-element-explorer.cfm/tab/data/deid/127

Wade, S. E., Fauske, J. R., & Thompson, A. (2008). Prospective teachers' problem solving in online peer-led dialogues. *American Educational Research Journal, 45,* 398–442.

Zacarian, D. (2013). *Mastering academic language: A framework for supporting student achievement.* Thousand Oaks, CA: Corwin.

Zacarian, D., & Haynes, J. (2012). *The essential guide for educating beginning English learners.* Thousand Oaks, CA: Corwin.

Index

CORWIN

A SAGE Company

Corwin is committed to improving education for all learners by publishing books and other professional development resources for those serving the field of PreK–12 education. By providing practical, hands-on materials, Corwin continues to carry out the promise of its motto: **"Helping Educators Do Their Work Better."**